We Don't Do Shame!

We Don't Do Shame!

How Belonging Heals What Addiction Breaks

under the supervision of
Ryan Canaday

Theological Essentials

©Digital Theological Library 2025
CC BY-NC-ND 4.0 International License
This work is licensed under a **Creative Commons Attribution–NonCommercial–NoDerivatives 4.0 International License (CC BY-NC-ND 4.0)**.
You are free to:

- **Share** — copy and redistribute the original DTL produced pdf.

Under the following terms:

- **Attribution** — You must give appropriate credit to the creator and the DTL Press.
- **NonCommercial** — You may not use the material for commercial purposes.
- **No Derivatives** — If you remix, transform, or build upon the material, you may not distribute the modified material.

Library of Congress Cataloging-in-Publication Data

Ryan Canaday (creator).
We Don't Do Shame: How Belonging Heals What Addiction Breaks / Ryan Canaday
126 + xi pp. cm. 12.7 x 20.32
ISBN 979-8-89731-988-6 (Print)
ISBN 979-8-89731-196-5 (Ebook)
ISBN 979-8-89731-208-5 (Kindle)
ISBN 979-8-89731-217-7 (Abridged Audio Discussion)
    1. Recovery movement—Religious aspects—Christianity
    2. Substance abuse—Religious aspects—Christianity.
    3. Church work with substance abusers.

BV4635 .C36 2025

This book is available in other languages at www.DTLPress.com

Cover Image: Created by Ryan Canaday, using AI.

Contents

Series Preface
vii

Author's Preface
xi

Introduction
1

Chapter 1
Addiction is the Wound Disguised as a Fix
5

Chapter 2
Families on the Frontline
15

Chapter 3
Not a Moral Failure
27

Chapter 4
Shame Is a Killer
35

Chapter 5
Speaking Real, Not Preachy
45

Chapter 6
Teaching Spiritual Wisdom Without Religious Baggage
53

Chapter 7
Listening as a Radical Act
63

Chapter 8
Helping the Wrecked Without Playing Savior
73

Chapter 9
The Language of Hope Without the BS
83

Chapter 10
Creating Space for Healing, Recovery, and Spiritual Connection
93

Chapter 11
Spaces of Radical Welcome
105

Chapter 12
Practices That Stick
111

Chapter 13
Staying in the Game for the Long Haul
119

Series Preface

Artificial Intelligence (AI) is changing everything, including theological scholarship and education. This series, *Theological Essentials*, is designed to bring the creative potential of AI to the field of theological education. In the traditional model, a scholar with both mastery of the scholarly discourse and a record of successful classroom teaching would spend several months—or even several years—writing, revising and rewriting an introductory text which would then be transferred to a publisher who also invested months or years in production processes. Even though the end product was typically quite predictable, this slow and expensive process caused the prices of textbooks to balloon. As a result, students in developed nations paid more than they should have for the books and students in developing nations typically had no access to these (cost-prohibitive) textbooks until they appeared as discards and donations decades later. In previous generations, the need for quality assurance—in the form of content generation, expert review, copy-editing and printing time—may have made this slow, expensive and exclusionary approach inevitable. However, AI is changing everything.

This series is very different; it is created by AI. The cover of each volume identifies the work as "created under the supervision of" an expert in the field. However, that person is not an author in the traditional sense. The creator of each volume has been trained by the DTL staff in the use of AI and *the creator has used AI to create, edit, revise and recreate the text that you see*. With that creation process clearly identified, let me explain the goals of this series.

Our Goals:

Credibility: Although AI has made—and continues to make—huge strides over the last few years, no unsupervised AI can create a truly reliable or fully credible college or seminary level text. The limitations of AI generated content sometimes originates from the limitations of the content itself (the training set may be inadequate), but more often, user dissatisfaction with AI-generated content arises from human errors associated with poor prompt engineering. The DTL Press has sought to overcome both of these problems by hiring established scholars with widely recognized expertise to create books within their areas of expertise and by training those scholars and experts in AI prompt engineering. To be clear, the scholar whose name appears on the cover of this work has created this volume—generating, reading, regenerating, rereading and revising the work. Even though the work was generated (in varying degrees) by AI, the names of our scholarly creators appear on the cover as a guarantee that the content is equally credible with any introductory work which that scholar/creator would pen using the traditional model.

Stability: AI is generative, meaning that the response to each prompt is uniquely generated for that specific request. No two AI-generated responses are precisely the same. The inevitable variability of AI responses presents a significant pedagogical challenge for professors and students who wish to begin their discussions and analysis on the basis of a shared set of ideas. Educational institutions need stable texts in order to prevent pedagogical chaos. These books provide that stable text from which to teach, discuss and engage ideas.

Affordability: The DTL Press is committed to the idea that affordability should not be a barrier to knowledge. *All persons are equally deserving of the right to know and to understand.* Therefore, ebook versions of all DTL Press books are available from the DTL libraries without charge, and available as print books for a nominal fee. Our scholar/creators are to be thanked for their willingness to forego traditional royalty arrangements. (Our creators are compensated for their generative work, but they do not receive royalties in the traditional sense.)

Accessibility: The DTL Press would like to make high quality, low cost introductory textbooks available to everyone, everywhere in the world. The books in this series are immediately made available in multiple languages. The DTL Press will create translations in other languages upon request. Translations are, of course, generated by AI.

Our Acknowledged Limitations:

Some readers are undoubtedly thinking, "but AI can only produce derivative scholarship; AI can't create original, innovative scholarship." That criticism is, of course, largely accurate. AI is largely limited to aggregating, organizing and repackaging pre-existing ideas (although sometimes in ways that can be used to accelerate and refine the production of original scholarship). Still while acknowledging this inherent limitation of AI, the DTL Press would offer two comments: (1) Introductory texts are seldom meant to be truly ground breaking in their originality and (2) the DTL Press has other series dedicated to publishing original scholarship with traditional authorship.

Our Invitation:

The DTL Press would like to fundamentally reshape academic publishing in the theological world to make scholarship more accessible and more affordable in two ways. First, we would like to generate introductory texts in all areas of theological discourse, so that no one is ever forced to "buy a textbook" in any language. It is our vision for professors anywhere to be able to use one book, two books or an entire set of books in this series as the *introductory* textbooks for their classes. Second, we would also like to publish traditionally authored scholarly monographs for Open Access (free) distribution for an advanced scholarly readership.

Finally, the DTL Press is non-confessional and will publish works in any area of religious studies. Traditionally authored books are peer-reviewed; AI-generated introductory book creation is open to anyone with the required expertise to supervise content generation in that area of discourse. If you share the DTL Press's commitment to credibility, affordability and accessibility, contact us about changing the world of theological publishing by contributing to this series or a more traditionally authored series.

With high expectations,
Thomas E. Phillips
DTL Press Executive Director
www.thedtl.org
www.DTLpress.com

Author's Preface

Some of the stories in this book are AI generated. They convey a broad scope of lived experience. All of them speak to the real life questions, doubts, struggles, and longings that encompass life in addiction and recovery, as well as the spiritual journey. Using AI in this way also helps protect anonymity while still telling the truth of the struggle.

Those battling addiction, and their loved ones battling alongside of them, often feel as if they are barely hanging on. There is a real sense of hopelessness and despair. The stories in these pages hold that tension honestly, but they also serve as a reminder that there is a way out of the chaos. Despair doesn't get the final word.

In my work, and in my recovery, I encounter stories like these on a regular basis.

Ryan

Introduction

"We Don't Do Shame"

"I'm Ryan. I'm an alcoholic."

Those were the scariest words I have ever said. The first time I spoke them, my voice shook, my palms sweated, and my chest felt like it might cave in. I did not want to be in that room. I did not want to admit what I had become. I was a pastor for crying out loud, how could I be the one with hidden vodka bottles and sleepless nights? My head spun with fear: What will they think? What if they do not let me back in? How did I let it get this bad?

When my turn came, I said the words anyway. And in that fragile moment, something shifted… but I was also terrified. The fear did not evaporate just because I spoke my truth. It sat heavy in my chest, reminding me of every failure and every doubt. And if you have ever been there, if you have ever said the hard thing, admitted the truth you were sure would destroy you, you know that fear. It is the kind that shakes you to your bones. And let me tell you: you are not crazy for feeling it, and you are not alone in it. Fear does not vanish overnight. But naming the truth is the first crack in shame's armor.

I felt like Jacob on the run, running from God, from my past, from myself. In Genesis, Jacob wrestles with God through the night and, when pressed, finally admits his own name: "I am Jacob." It is as if God says, Good. Now we can work with the truth. On the first morning I said, "I'm Ryan. I'm an alcoholic," it was like saying my name again for the first time. It was like God whispered, Good. We have got some work to do, but you are not alone anymore.

By grace and the guidance of people who refused to let shame have the last word, I have been sober since January 7, 2013. God removed from me the obsession of the drink, but God did not do it with lightning bolts or perfect speeches. God did it through honest conversation, imperfect people, and a community of other addicts and alcoholics in recovery that made space for me.

That is why FREE Recovery Community exists. We built FREE because too many addicts, loved ones of addicts, and spiritual refugees have been driven into silence, ashamed, judged, or made to feel they did not belong. FREE is a place where we break the silence of addiction, create space for healing and recovery, and make room for spiritual connection. We do not gather to perform religion or protect tradition. We gather because nobody should have to walk through hell alone.

Let me pause here to define a term you will hear throughout this book: spiritual refugees. Spiritual refugees are people who have been kicked around by religion, hurt, excluded, or shamed by faith communities. They feel like they do not belong anywhere near "church," yet many still carry a longing for connection, grace, and meaning. Some did not walk away out of anger, they were shoved out by hypocrisy, judgment, or silence. They are searching for God but terrified of the places that claim to represent God.

This book is for four groups of people:
- The addict who is desperate for a way out but terrified to speak their truth.
- The loved one of an addict who has cried, bargained, and screamed at the ceiling, wondering if anything will ever change.
- The spiritual refugee who was hurt by religion, or who has never set foot in a faith space but longs for something bigger than the pain.
- The leader who wants to have honest conversations but does not know where to begin. You want to love addicts, their families, and spiritual refugees, but you are terrified of saying the wrong thing or not having the answers.

You will not find easy answers here. You will find raw talk about addiction and shame, about community and grace, about setting boundaries, about doubt, about laughter and tears and second chances. You will find stories from FREE: standing ovations for broken people, cups of coffee that save lives, and Saturday nights where recovering addicts, weary parents, and spiritual wanderers sit side by side. But you will also find stories beyond FREE, real, unpolished glimpses into the battles people face with addiction, the pain their loved ones carry, and the quiet courage it takes to keep showing up when nothing seems to be changing. These stories are not sanitized or safe; they are real because this fight is real.

What you hold in your hands is not just a book. It is an invitation. An invitation to lay down the crushing weight of shame. To step out of silence. To risk honest conversation. To build spaces where grace outruns judgment.

Here is what I know: God is not threatened by your questions. God is not repulsed by your wreckage. God is not standing at a distance with arms crossed, waiting for you to get it together. God is already here, running toward you through the mess, through the wreckage, whispering, You are not alone. You have always belonged.

So come as you are, the broken, the searching, the angry, the sober, the relapsing, the hopeful, the skeptical. Let us talk through the wreckage together. Let us choose connection over isolation. Let us choose grace over shame. Because here is the truth that will echo through every chapter of this book and through every corner of FREE: We don't do shame.

Chapter 1
Addiction is the Wound Disguised as a Fix

The Ache Beneath the Surface

Addiction does not stroll into a life wearing a name tag. It sneaks in quietly, sometimes dressed as relief, sometimes disguised as celebration. For many, the first drink or hit feels like oxygen after years of choking. It works, at first. The anxiety softens. The shame quiets. The loneliness eases. What begins as relief becomes routine. Routine hardens into need. Need becomes the cage. Addiction is rarely about the substance itself. It is about an ache, a wound beneath the surface, that demands soothing.

Addiction does not discriminate. It threads its way through every zip code, bank account, and faith tradition. It grips blue-collar workers and CEOs, devoted churchgoers and spiritual skeptics, parents and their children. It does not care about your résumé, your morals, or the size of your house. Addiction is an equal-opportunity thief, and that truth shatters the myth that "people like us" are safe from its reach.

And to the addict reading this: I see the war you have been fighting. The nights staring at a ceiling at 3 a.m., your heart pounding like a drum you cannot silence. The mornings you swore today would be different, only to watch the bottle or the needle win again by lunchtime. The mirrors you have avoided because they tell a story you cannot bear to face. The quiet begging you have done, pleading with God, with the universe, with anyone who might listen, to make it stop. It feels like drowning in plain sight, like screaming underwater while the world keeps walking by. This is not weakness or a lack of love for your family. This is a brutal, bone-deep battle for your life. And even if you feel invisible, your fight is seen, and you are not alone.

And to the loved one of the addict: you know this fight too, don't you? You have paced floors at 2 a.m., rehearsing the perfect words that might finally break through. You have driven past bars or sketchy motels, scanning the parking lot for their car, your stomach twisted into knots. You have stared at your phone, willing it to ring, not knowing if silence means safety or disaster. You have cried in showers so no one would hear, screamed into steering wheels, and worn a smile at work while your insides burned. You have prayed prayers that sounded more like bargaining or begging, and you have cursed God when nothing changed. You carry their chaos in your own body: the clenched jaw, the shallow breathing, the exhaustion that never ends. This is not just their war; it has become yours. And you are not weak for feeling broken. You are a warrior holding hope on their behalf, even when your hands are shaking.

Beneath that ache is often something even deeper: spiritual disconnection. It is the hollow place where we feel cut off from everything meaningful, from God, from others, from our own selves. Addiction often points to this spiritual disconnection, a desperate attempt to fill an emptiness that substances can never satisfy. The goal is not just to stop using; it is to find our way back to connection, to life, to love, to presence.

The Myth We Tell Ourselves

We crave simple stories about complicated pain. They are neat. They let us pretend the world is fair and manageable. So when it comes to addiction, we repeat myths that sound safe, but they are lies that keep us from seeing what is real. These myths don't just distort reality, they build walls between us and healing. They allow us to point fingers instead of extending hands. They let us stay comfortable rather than confront the discomfort of messy truth. When we cling to these myths, we stop asking deeper questions. We stop listening. We distance ourselves from the people who are suffering. And maybe most dangerously, we cut ourselves off from the possibility of compassion, the very thing that can break shame's power and begin the work of restoration. If we want to heal, as individuals, families, and communities, the myths have to fall.

Myth #1: Addiction happens to other people.

We tell ourselves it is the man under the bridge or the woman whose mugshot flashes on the news. But addiction walks into living rooms with family photos on the wall. It slips into suburban kitchens, corner offices, and church pews. It does not check income brackets or Sunday attendance records. Pretending addiction is far away protects us from facing its proximity, maybe even its fingerprints in our own families.

Myth #2: Addiction is a moral failure.

It is easier to believe people drink or use because they are weak or reckless. If it is just bad choices, then we do not have to face the harder truth: addiction rewires brains. It hijacks dopamine pathways and decision-making. It feeds on trauma, stress, and shame. Labeling it a moral collapse might make us feel righteous, but it leaves the wounded abandoned.

Myth #3: If you really loved us, you would stop.

This one devastates families. It suggests that continued use equals a lack of love. But the person drinking or using often loves their people desperately, yet love alone does not override a brain caught in a craving-relief-shame cycle. They are not choosing the bottle or the needle over their family. They are losing an internal war most outsiders cannot see.

Myth #4: If your faith were strong enough, this would not happen.

Some churches have preached this myth, turning prayer into performance and God into a cruel accountant. Spiritual refugees carry scars from hearing, "Just pray harder" or "Confess more." When healing does not come instantly, they walk away believing grace has limits. But the failure is not theirs, it is the myth itself. Grace does not abandon people in detox centers or dark alleys. Grace does not demand perfection before offering love. These myths persist because they are comforting. They keep the world simple, blame tidy, and distance intact. But reality is messier and far more hopeful. Addiction is not a verdict on a person's worth. It is a flashing signal of pain and a call for compassion. When we dismantle the myths, we make space for honest conversations, better support, and the kind of community that can save lives.

Story
The Kitchen Table

On a rainy Tuesday night, Megan sat at her kitchen table staring at her son's empty chair. He was twenty-eight, brilliant with a guitar, and two months into another bender. She whispered to herself the old refrain: "If he really loved me, he would stop." It was easier to believe that than to admit she felt powerless. Easier than facing the fear that nothing she said could make him walk back through the door sober. Weeks later, she found herself at an open recovery meeting, dragged there by a friend who had said, "Just sit and listen." A middle-aged man with trembling hands spoke: "I loved my family more than my own life. But when the craving hit, love was not enough to stop me. I was not choosing the bottle over my kids, I was drowning, and I did not know how to swim."

Megan felt the myth crack. Tears came, not of shame this time, but of release. For the first time, she saw her son not as a betrayer, but as a wounded man in a cage his mind had built. She could not pry the bars apart for him. But she could start loving him without the lie that he was drinking at her. She could reach out for support, learn to set boundaries without blame, and speak to him from a place of compassion rather than accusation. That night, Megan did not get a miracle phone call. Her son did not walk in the door sober. But something in her shifted. The wreckage was still real, but so was hope.

Why Naming the Wound Matters

We cannot heal what we refuse to name. Pretending addiction is "just a phase" or "a string of bad choices" keeps everyone trapped, both the one using and the ones who love them. Denial is seductive because it buys temporary comfort. But every day spent denying is a day the wound festers. Naming the wound is not about labeling someone as hopeless or excusing destructive behavior. It is about telling the truth in a world that thrives on half-truths. When we name addiction for what it is, a deep wound wrapped in chemicals and cravings, we shift the battlefield. Instead of fighting the person, we fight despair. Instead of shaming the addict, we shame the stigma.

"We are only as sick as our secrets."

Families often avoid naming the wound out of fear: fear that saying "addiction" out loud makes it real, fear of gossip, fear of watching hope crumble. But silence does not protect hope. It starves it. Speaking the truth, "My partner is drinking again," "My daughter is using," breaks the spell of secrecy. It opens the door to support groups, therapy, recovery communities, and honest prayers that do not pretend everything is fine. Naming the wound allows everyone involved to breathe, even when the air still smells like smoke. For spiritual refugees, naming the wound is even more complicated. Many have been told that to admit addiction is to admit personal failure or spiritual weakness. Reclaiming your voice, saying, "This is addiction, and it is not my moral collapse." is an act of holy rebellion against the myths that harmed you.

The Path Toward Hope

Hope is not a lightning strike or a polished testimony. It does not explode into your life with fireworks or arrive wrapped in certainty. For many addicts and their loved ones, hope feels impossible, like a language you have forgotten how to speak. Maybe you are reading this while wondering if anything can ever change. Maybe you have buried friends, broken promises, or burned bridges, and you fear hope is for other people. Hear this: your story is not over. Hope may not kick the door down, but it will slip quietly into the cracks if you let it. It shows up in small, unremarkable ways that save lives: the trembling voice that asks for help, the unexpected text that says, "I'm thinking of you," the stranger who sees your pain and doesn't look away. To the addict barely holding on, hope is not just a concept, it is oxygen. To the loved one exhausted and afraid, it is the thin thread that keeps you from despair. It is not a prize for the deserving but a lifeline for the desperate. Even here, in the wreckage, hope is still reaching for you.

"One day at a time."

Hope grows in community. Isolation feeds addiction. Connection starves it. This does not mean pretending everything is fine or tolerating harm. It means showing up honestly, messy, afraid, but present. Recovery meetings, therapy circles, trusted friends, even strangers with coffee-stained paper cups become sacred spaces when people choose to show up and tell the truth. Surrender is the paradoxical doorway. Not surrender to defeat, but surrender to reality: "I cannot control this alone." This is the first step of the 12 Steps for a reason. Control is the drug beneath the drug. Families try to manage outcomes, addicts try to manage cravings, and both end up exhausted. Surrender does not guarantee instant change, but it creates the conditions where change is possible. It cracks the cage of the mind, letting light in. For spiritual refugees, hope often comes from unexpected places: a neighbor's kindness, a recovery slogan scribbled on a bathroom wall, a moment of stillness in nature. It may not look like the faith you left behind, but that does not make it any less holy. Hope is not a distant prize for the perfect. It is a present companion for the broken. As we move deeper into this book, you will discover that hope is not a clean, linear path. It zigzags through relapse, disappointment, laughter, and small victories. It requires courage to keep showing up, to keep talking, and to keep choosing connection over silence. Even here, in the wreckage, hope is alive, and it is speaking life if we are willing to listen.

    Megan's story is not unique. It is the quiet reality behind countless closed doors. For every person battling a substance, there is a web of parents, partners, siblings, and friends holding their breath, bargaining with God, or replaying arguments in their heads. Addiction does not just wound the one drinking or using. It splashes pain across the whole circle. And too often, families are told to either rescue recklessly or detach completely, as if those are the only options. But there is another way: a path of loving fiercely without losing yourself. In the next chapter, we will step into the chaos that addiction creates for families and explore how they can find their own healing, even when the outcomes stay uncertain.

Reflection Questions for Chapter 1

Myth-Busting Your Own Story: Which of the myths about addiction ("It happens to other people," "It is a moral failure," "If you loved us you would stop," or "Faith should have fixed this") have you believed or spoken? How has holding onto that myth shaped your attitude toward yourself or someone you love?

Facing the Wound: When you think about the metaphor of addiction as "a wound disguised as a fix," what memories, feelings, or personal experiences does that stir up for you? Where might denial or silence have kept you (or your family) from naming the wound honestly?

Seeing the Wreckage Without Losing Hope: Megan's story did not end in a miracle phone call. Where in your life have you been tempted to equate immediate outcomes with hope? What small, gritty signs of life, however imperfect, might you be overlooking right now?

Choosing Surrender Over Control: Control is called "the drug beneath the drug." In what area of your life, whether you are the one using or the one loving someone who uses, might surrender open a doorway to healing or connection? What would surrender look like in practice for you today?

Chapter 2
Families on the Frontline
Loving Without Losing Yourself

The Phone Call No Parent Wants

Linda was folding laundry when the phone rang. It was 2:13 a.m. Her stomach clenched before she even picked up. The voice on the other end, an ER nurse, was calm but firm. Her son, twenty-four years old, had been found unconscious in the bathroom of a gas station. He was alive, but barely. As the nurse spoke, Linda stared at a pile of clean towels on the floor. Hours earlier she had been imagining her son's future: marriage, kids, Sunday dinners. Now, all she could think was, Please, God, don't let him die tonight.

On the drive to the hospital, Linda's husband gripped the steering wheel so tightly his knuckles turned white. Neither spoke. They had said all the words before, pleading, threats, promises, prayers screamed into the ceiling. They had tried everything they knew to keep their son safe: locking up credit cards, tracking his phone, begging him to go back to rehab. Each new tactic felt like holding back the tide with a broom. In that moment, Linda realized something she could barely admit: her love could not out-muscle his addiction.

Loving Someone Who Is Drowning

Loving an addict feels like living on a fault line. The ground shifts without warning. One day you get a text saying they are clean and hopeful. The next day, silence or another crisis. Families become hypervigilant, scanning for danger, rehearsing speeches, making plans to save someone who does not always want to be saved. The emotional whiplash leaves bruises no one sees.

The guilt can be crushing. You replay every memory, searching for the single mistake that set this in motion: the argument you should not have had, the warning signs you missed, the moment you should have said "no." You wonder if you are a bad parent, partner, or sibling. You wonder if your love was not enough. That guilt creeps into every corner of your life, your work, your friendships, even your sleep. It whispers that if you had just loved them better, prayed harder, or been stronger, things would not be this way.

Over time, loving the addict can start to feel like its own addiction. You check their social media at midnight, drive by places they might be using, and wait for your phone to light up with news, good or bad, because even bad news feels better than the silence. You cancel your plans to rescue them, cover their debts, or clean up another mess because the idea of doing nothing feels unbearable. The rush of relief when they are safe can be intoxicating, and the crash when they relapse is devastating. Without meaning to, you begin to orbit their chaos. Their highs and lows become your own.

This cycle is exhausting and unsustainable. The pain you carry is real, raw, jagged, and heavy. It can feel like it has taken up residence in your chest, stealing your breath and hollowing out your joy. It can fracture marriages, isolate you from friends, and make you doubt your own worth. But hear this: your pain is not permanent, and it is not the whole story. There is a way out, not a quick fix or an easy answer, but a path that begins with releasing what you cannot control, finding support, and tending to your own wounds. You do not have to disappear into their chaos or be consumed by despair. Healing is possible for you, too. You are not broken beyond repair, and you are not alone in this fight.

The Myth of Total Responsibility

Many loved ones secretly believe that if they just did more, prayed harder, loved better, enforced tougher rules, they could fix their person. This belief is seductive because it feels like control in a world spinning out of control. But it is a dangerous illusion. Total responsibility for another person's addiction can quietly destroy families. It erodes marriages, pits siblings against each other, and leaves parents drowning in guilt.

This myth is often fed by cultural and even religious messages that glorify self-sacrifice: "Good parents don't give up," "A faithful spouse never stops fighting," "If you really loved them, you'd save them." But saving someone is not the same as loving them. Addiction is not a math equation where more effort guarantees a solution. You cannot attend every meeting for them, detox in their place, or choose sobriety on their behalf.

Taking on total responsibility traps you in a cycle of panic and exhaustion. You might cancel plans, hide your loved one's behavior from friends, or drain savings accounts to pay for quick fixes, only to feel the crushing weight of failure when relapse happens anyway. This pattern does not heal your loved one. It only deepens your own wounds and fuels resentment on both sides. Resentment builds slowly: you start feeling bitter toward the addict for "ruining everything," and they begin to resent you for micromanaging their life, even as they depend on your help. It poisons communication, every conversation becomes a landmine. The addict may lash out in anger or shame, while the loved one grows cold, sarcastic, or withdrawn. Over time, the relationship can become defined not by love, but by unspoken blame and silent anger.

Resentment is a thief, it steals tenderness, erodes trust, and isolates everyone involved. Breaking free from the myth of total responsibility does not mean you stop caring or turn away from your loved one. It means you step out of the cycle that keeps wounding you both. It means you choose honesty over control, and compassion over bitterness. It means you allow space for your loved one to take responsibility for their recovery while you take responsibility for your own healing. This shift does not happen overnight, but it is the first step toward relationships rooted in dignity rather than despair.

Boundaries Are Not Betrayal

Boundaries are often misunderstood as rejection or punishment. In reality, they are the opposite: they are a fierce, intentional form of love. A boundary says, "I will not disappear into your chaos, but I will remain here as my whole self, offering love without losing myself."

Setting boundaries is not easy. It is normal to feel guilt, fear, or second-guess yourself. Most of us were never taught how to hold a line without shame or anger, and when it involves someone you love deeply, it can feel almost impossible. Struggling with boundaries does not mean you are weak or unloving. It means you are human. The discomfort you feel is a sign of how much you care, not proof that boundaries are wrong.

Without boundaries, families can become extensions of the addiction, covering for lies, paying debts, making excuses, or tolerating harm. Over time, everyone in the household starts living in survival mode, tiptoeing around explosions and carrying shame that does not belong to them.

Healthy boundaries stop the addiction from consuming the whole family. They draw lines that protect emotional, physical, and financial safety. They also send a powerful, unspoken message: "Your addiction is not the total truth of who you are, but it also does not get to control my life."

Examples of boundaries in action:

"I love you and will listen, but I will not be spoken to with threats or insults."

"You cannot stay here if you are actively using, but I will help you find a meeting or shelter."

"I will not give you money, but I will pick you up from treatment."

Boundaries are not betrayal. They are a way of loving without enabling. They create room for accountability and dignity. They may cause anger at first. Addicts often test boundaries to see if the old patterns will return. Hold firm. Over time, boundaries can become the framework where trust, honesty, and real healing take root.

Boundaries can also be confused with shame. When you hold a line, the one receiving it might kick, scream, and lash out like a child who feels cornered. They may accuse you of abandoning them or not loving them enough. This reaction is part of the chaos addiction creates, it is not evidence that you are shaming them. Shame says, "You are worthless." A boundary says, "You are valuable, but I will not let your chaos destroy us both." It is critical to remember the difference. Holding boundaries is an act of dignity and love, not humiliation or condemnation.

Finding Your Own Recovery

The 12-Step wisdom says, "Family members need recovery, too," and it is true. Groups like Al-Anon or Nar-Anon exist not to fix the addict, but to help families heal their own wounds. Therapy, trusted friendships, and spiritual practices can also offer a lifeline.

But 12-step programs are not the only way. There are other strong and meaningful recovery paths, faith-based communities, secular support groups, therapy-centered models, and alternative recovery fellowships. What matters is not finding the "right" branded path but finding the path that truly helps you heal and connect. The key is to explore what works for you and your family and to remember that you are not locked into a single method.

For spiritual refugees, those who have been harmed by religion and carry heavy baggage, this journey can be especially complicated. Many have been told by religious authorities that their pain is a result of weak faith or moral failure. They may flinch at words like "God" or "church" because those words are tied to wounds instead of comfort. To the spiritual refugee: your hesitation makes sense. Your struggle with trust is not rebellion or bitterness, it is the scar tissue of past harm. This book sees you. It honors the weight you carry and invites you to seek healing without shame or pressure.

Spiritual refugees may have to unlearn harmful religious messages to accept this help. You may have been told that self-care is selfish or that love means endless sacrifice. But healthy love includes caring for yourself. Your pain matters. Your story matters. And you cannot pour from an empty cup.

Speaking Hope Without Illusions

Loving someone with an addiction means learning to hold two truths at once: the reality of the wreckage and the possibility of redemption. Hope is not a fairy tale ending or blind optimism. It is the quiet decision to believe that change is possible even when the evidence feels thin. It is the refusal to let despair dictate the final chapter.

True hope acknowledges relapse, disappointment, and heartbreak. It does not sugarcoat the pain or erase the boundaries you must hold. Instead, it whispers: "Even here, something good can still grow."

For the spiritual but not religious, this kind of hope is not about dogma. It is about connection. It is the sacred spark that flickers even when you do not trust churches or preachers or tidy answers. And if you carry resentment toward religion or those who used faith as a weapon, your pain is valid. The wounds you feel are real. You may have been judged, excluded, or told you were unworthy, and now even words like "God" or "prayer" taste bitter on your tongue. That pain does not disqualify you from grace, it points to how deeply you long for something true.

Letting go does not mean pretending none of it hurt. It does not erase the betrayal or the anger. It means choosing not to let resentment be the loudest voice in your life. Sometimes moving forward requires laying down what poisoned you, not to excuse it, but to keep it from defining you. You may have to let go of old images of God that were too small or cruel, the ones that told you you'd never measure up. You may have to bury some of the lies you were handed so that something new can live. That is not weakness, it is courageous, soul-deep work.

Real hope sounds like:

"I believe you can recover, even if you stumble."

"I will love you, but I will not enable your addiction."

"You are not defined by your worst day."

"Even if religion hurt you, God has not abandoned you; there is still a place for you to belong."

"Your pain as a loved one matters, and you are allowed to heal even while they are still struggling."

Choosing to Love Fiercely and Let Go

Linda's son survived that night. He would relapse again before finding lasting recovery. Linda and her husband joined an Al-Anon group, where they learned to stop policing every moment and start tending to their own hearts. They discovered that loving fiercely does not mean losing yourself. It means offering compassion without surrendering your sanity, showing up without sacrificing your soul.

Relapse does not have to be part of everyone's story. Some people find recovery and never return to using. But the reality is that for many who struggle with addiction, relapse is often part of the journey. A setback does not erase progress or worth. It is not proof of hopelessness. It is evidence of how powerful addiction can be and how much support and persistence recovery requires. For families, this truth is painful. It can feel like betrayal or failure. But relapse can also be a teacher: a reminder that healing is rarely linear and that hope cannot depend solely on uninterrupted success.

Choosing to love fiercely and let go means releasing the illusion that your control or their perfect performance determines the future. That illusion feels safe, like a lifeline in a storm; you cling to it because letting go feels like stepping off a cliff with no parachute. It whispers that if you just check their texts, search their car, or make the right threat, you can steer the outcome. It promises that your vigilance will be enough to keep them alive. But the hard, heartbreaking truth is that control is a mirage. You can beg, bargain, police, and plead, and still watch them relapse. You can lose yourself in their chaos and still not save them. The fear of letting go is real, and it cuts deep. It feels like betrayal, like you are abandoning them in their darkest hour. But letting go is not giving up, it is the brave act of refusing to drown alongside them. It is standing on the shore with your heart wide open, saying, "I will love you, but I cannot swim for you." When you loosen your grip, you make space for grace, for community, and for the possibility that they will learn to swim on their own. Letting go is terrifying, but it is the only way to stop the addiction from swallowing you whole.

If you are a parent, spouse, sibling, or friend on the frontlines, hear this: you are not alone. You are not failing because you cannot fix them. Your love is not wasted. You can care deeply and still step back. And even in the chaos, even when the outcomes are uncertain, there is hope, for them, and for you.

As we move forward, Chapter 3 will take us inside the mind of addiction itself: why it is not a moral failure but an obsession of the mind, a cage that only surrender and connection can begin to unlock.

Reflection Questions for Chapter 2

Boundaries and Love: Think about a time when setting or even considering a boundary felt unbearable or "unloving." What emotions (fear, guilt, anger) did that stir in you? How might reframing boundaries as an act of love rather than rejection begin to change the way you view them?

Hope Without Guarantees: Reflect on a moment when hope felt impossible. What helped you hold on, however faintly, to the idea that healing or change could still be possible? How does viewing hope as a steady, quiet decision rather than a perfect outcome reframe your expectations?

Facing the Reality of Relapse: Relapse does not erase progress, but its pain is real. How do you reconcile the heartbreak of setbacks with the truth that recovery is rarely linear? What would it look like to respond to relapse with both honesty and compassion, for yourself and for your loved one?

Your Own Healing Journey: Consider your own need for healing apart from your loved one's choices. Where might you need to release control, seek support, or practice self-care? What concrete step could you take this week (joining a group, reaching out to a friend, or simply resting) to honor your own recovery?

Chapter 3
Not a Moral Failure
When the Mind Becomes the Cage

The Successful Man No One Suspected

Marcus was the kind of guy people envied. A steady job, a smiling family in Christmas photos, and a volunteer spot at the local food pantry. He was the guy who remembered birthdays and showed up early to help friends move. No one saw the whiskey hidden behind paint cans in the garage. No one knew about the mornings he threw up in the shower or the nights he stared at the ceiling, promising himself he would stop tomorrow. Marcus was not a bad guy. He was not weak, lazy, or reckless. He was drowning in a cage built inside his own mind, a cage no one else could see.

When his wife found the bottles, her first words were, "How could you do this to us?" Marcus felt the shame crash over him like a tidal wave. He wanted to explain that he hated it too, that every sip felt like both relief and self-betrayal. But shame stole his voice. Like so many others, he carried the unspoken belief that addiction was proof of his moral failure.

The Lie of Moral Failure

Society loves a clean story: good people make good choices and bad people make bad ones. Addiction blows that story apart. Addiction is not a simple choice to do wrong. It is not evidence of weak character or a broken moral compass. Addiction is an obsession of the mind, a rewiring of the brain's reward system that traps even the strongest, kindest, most principled people.

For generations, addiction has been labeled as a character flaw, a weakness, or a deliberate choice to self-destruct. We have used shame as a weapon, believing it might scare people into changing. We have whispered about the "drunk uncle," gossiped about the "junkie down the street," and shaken our heads as if the moral superiority in our disapproval could heal someone's pain. But this lie, that addiction is a moral failure, has wrecked lives. It has pushed people deeper into secrecy, made them afraid to ask for help, and convinced them they are beyond redemption. The truth is simpler and harder: addiction is not about being a bad person. Addiction is what happens when a wounded mind is hijacked by craving and compulsion.

Moral failure suggests there is an easy fix: just be better, try harder, resist temptation. But anyone who has battled addiction or loved someone who has knows it is not that simple. The person you love may want to stop desperately. They may be terrified of what they are doing to themselves and others. But their mind has been hijacked. Telling them to just quit is like telling someone locked in a cage to just walk out.

When the Mind Becomes the Cage

Addiction is not only a habit or a string of bad decisions. It is a neurological takeover. Substances flood the brain with dopamine, the chemical messenger for pleasure and reward. At first, this feels like relief: the anxiety quiets, the sadness lifts, the emptiness fills. But over time, the brain adapts. The normal pathways for joy and motivation dull, leaving only one door open: the substance. This shift is not a moral collapse; it is a biological one.

As the brain's chemistry changes, willpower alone becomes like a paper key against iron bars. Even when someone truly wants to stop, the brain screams for survival: Get more. Do whatever it takes. This is why people will risk jobs, relationships, even freedom, because their nervous system has been rewired to treat the substance as essential to life. The cage is invisible, but its bars are strong: cravings, triggers, fear of withdrawal, and the deep shame that convinces them they are beyond saving.

The cage tightens further because addiction hijacks memory and decision-making. The mind begins to rewrite reality: "I can handle just one," "It's not that bad," "Tomorrow will be different." These rationalizations are not conscious lies; they are the brain's desperate attempt to justify what its chemistry demands.

For family members, this can be maddening to watch. From the outside, it looks like betrayal or indifference. From the inside, it feels like drowning while pretending to swim. Marcus once described it this way: "It was not that I did not care about my family. I cared so much it hurt. But my brain would start screaming, and the bottle felt like the only way to make it stop. I hated it even as I reached for it."

Understanding addiction as a cage does not excuse harmful behavior. But it reframes the battle. It shifts the story from bad choices by a bad person to a sick mind that needs healing and connection. Recognizing the cage is the first step toward opening its door.

Breaking the Shame Cycle

Shame feeds addiction. It convinces people they are unworthy of help. It tells them they do not deserve a second chance or a tenth. But here is the truth: you cannot shame someone into wholeness. And you cannot shame yourself into recovery either. Healing begins when shame is replaced with honesty and connection.

If you are reading this and you know the battle of shame, the late-night promises to quit, the mornings you swore today would be different, the hidden bottles or needles you swore would be the last, you are not defective. You are not broken beyond repair. Shame wants to keep you silent because silence keeps you trapped. It whispers that you have already failed too many times to try again. But shame is a liar. Trying again is not weakness. It is defiance against the voice that says you are hopeless.

Some of you have walked into a meeting or opened up to a friend before, only to retreat when you stumbled again. You may think, "I've burned all my bridges." But bridges can be rebuilt. The people who matter, the ones who understand recovery, know that healing is rarely linear. They know relapse and setbacks happen, but they also know recovery is possible. You have not run out of chances.

Breaking shame's hold starts small. It might be a text to a trusted friend: "I'm not okay." It might be showing up at a support group and saying nothing at first, just listening. It might even be whispering your truth to yourself in the mirror: "I am not my worst day. I am not my addiction."

For the family member, it means refusing to use shame as a weapon. It means remembering that addiction is not proof of moral collapse. Speaking compassion does not excuse harm, but it creates space for change. It says, "I see your humanity even when I cannot accept your behavior."

Shame dies in the light of connection. You may feel unworthy of that light, but worthiness is not a prerequisite for healing. Connection does not wait for you to be perfect. It meets you in the wreckage, right where you are.

The Spiritual Dimension
Surrender and Connection

For spiritual refugees, the word "surrender" may sound like a trap. Religion may have been used against you, weaponizing shame or demanding blind obedience. But surrender in recovery is different. It is not groveling before a punishing god. It is an act of courage: admitting that control is an illusion and that healing requires help outside yourself.

If you are barely hanging on, this is for you: surrender does not mean giving up on life or resigning yourself to despair. It means loosening your white-knuckled grip on the illusion that you can fix this alone. It means acknowledging the truth you have been too exhausted to say out loud: "I need help." That is not weakness. That is the bravest sentence you may ever speak.

Surrender might look like picking up the phone even when your pride screams not to. It might be sitting in a recovery meeting with arms crossed, silently daring someone to prove that hope is real. It could be as simple as sitting under a dark sky, whispering to the universe or to a power you are not sure exists, "Please meet me here. Please show me a way forward."

Connection, too, can feel dangerous when you have been hurt, judged, or abandoned. To risk connection after betrayal takes incredible courage. But isolation is addiction's favorite weapon. Even a single honest conversation, a sponsor answering your call, a friend sitting with you without judgment, can break a crack in the darkness. You do not have to join a church or adopt someone else's beliefs to step into connection. You only have to take one small step out of the shadows and toward another human being.

If you are reading this and thinking you have already failed too many times to try again, hear this: you are not beyond reach. The wreckage is not the end of your story. Surrender and connection are not about perfection. They are about refusing to disappear, even when the shame and exhaustion tell you to give up. Love, grace, and the shared human spirit are still bigger than your worst moment, and they are waiting, even here, even now.

Hope Beyond the Cage

Picture this: a man who once woke up every day with trembling hands now wakes to the sound of his daughter's laughter drifting down the hallway. The same kitchen where he once hid bottles is now where he makes pancakes on Saturday mornings. This is what life outside the cage can look like.

Hope does not always feel like a roaring fire. Sometimes it is a fragile spark that you can barely see through the smoke. You might not feel hopeful right now, you may even feel numb or convinced that hope is for other people. But hope is real even when you cannot feel it. It is working quietly in places you cannot yet see: in the brain that can heal and rewire, in the relationships that can be mended, in the future you cannot yet imagine. Hope is stubborn like that. It survives your disbelief.

Life outside the cage is not perfect, but it is profoundly different. Outside the cage, mornings can bring peace instead of panic. Trust, once shattered, can slowly be rebuilt. Laughter can return to rooms that have been silent for years. You begin to remember what joy feels like without the fog of shame or the chemical shortcut of a drink or a hit. Simple moments, holding your child's hand, sharing a meal without fear, waking up without regret, become sacred. Outside the cage, you are free to build a future that is not defined by addiction's demands but by love, purpose, and presence. Even if you cannot see that future yet, it is still possible, and hope is already pulling you toward it.

Some people find freedom through 12-step recovery, others through therapy, alternative programs, or a combination of approaches. What matters is not fitting someone else's mold, but finding what works and walking that road one step at a time.

Marcus eventually entered treatment, not because shame cornered him, but because honesty and connection cracked the cage. He sat in a circle of strangers and heard a man say, "You're not a bad person. You're a sick person getting well." The words broke something loose inside him. They named what shame could not: addiction was not a verdict on his character. It was a wound in need of healing.

Reflection Questions for Chapter 3

Think of a time when shame shaped how you viewed yourself or someone you love. How did that shame impact your ability to seek or offer help?

In what ways have you or others believed the lie that addiction is a moral failure? How has that belief affected your relationships or recovery journey?

What does surrender mean to you, not in a religious sense, but as a courageous step toward honesty and connection?

Imagine the cage described in this chapter. What bars, fear, pride, shame, isolation, might need to crack in your life for hope to enter?

Chapter 4
Shame Is a Killer

The Basement Meeting

Jenna sat in her car outside a church basement, hands gripping the steering wheel until her knuckles ached. The sign on the door read "Recovery Meeting – All Welcome," but her mind was a storm of accusations. They'll judge you. You don't belong here. You're a failure, again.

Earlier that day, she overheard her cousin murmur on the phone, "Jenna's a lost cause." The words didn't just sting; they cut through the thin layer of hope she had left. But the shame ran deeper than her family's disappointment. Jenna felt abandoned by God. Growing up in a strict religious home, she had been taught that good Christians didn't stumble like this. She could still hear the voice of an old youth pastor: "Sin separates you from God." Sitting alone in the car, she believed it, believed that her relapse wasn't just proof of weakness but proof that even heaven had turned its back.

Tears blurred her vision as she gripped the wheel harder. She wanted to pray but couldn't find words that didn't sound hollow. She imagined God shaking His head in disgust, arms folded, unwilling to hear another empty promise. The idea of walking into a church basement felt like a cruel joke. What business did she have stepping inside God's house after breaking every vow she had made?

She almost turned the key in the ignition to drive away. But something, maybe defiance, maybe desperation, made her open the car door instead. She walked in, eyes fixed on the floor, bracing herself for the cold stares she was sure would come.

Instead, she heard a man share about his own relapse. He spoke plainly, his voice trembling but unapologetic: "I messed up. I hated myself. I thought God was done with me. But I'm here." The room didn't condemn him. It leaned in. Quiet nods. Soft "me too's." One woman reached over and squeezed his hand.

Something cracked in Jenna's chest. For the first time in months, she felt a flicker of warmth, small, fragile, but real. It wasn't that all her shame vanished in that moment, or that her perception of God healed overnight. But for the first time, she wondered if shame had been lying to her. Maybe God wasn't disgusted with her. Maybe the God she'd been told about, the one who keeps score, wasn't the whole story. Maybe grace was bigger than the wreckage.

What Shame Does to Addicts and Families

Shame is not just an unpleasant emotion, it is corrosive, suffocating, and cruel. It crawls into the deepest parts of your identity and rewrites the script about who you are. If you are someone caught in addiction, shame insists, This isn't something you did, this is who you are. Broken. Hopeless. Unworthy. It tells you that no matter how many times you try, the failure will define you. Even when you muster the courage to reach out, shame interrupts: Don't bother. They'll just see what a disappointment you are.

For families, shame is equally devastating. It convinces parents that they are bad mothers or fathers, spouses that they are somehow defective partners, siblings that their family is permanently marked by failure. Shame isolates whole households, keeping them silent when they most need support. Parents stop talking to friends, terrified of being judged. Spouses withdraw from community, not wanting to answer questions about another missed shift or another trip to rehab. Children internalize unspoken pain, growing up believing that secrets are safer than truth.

Shame doesn't just wound, it builds walls. It breaks trust, not only between loved ones but inside the heart of the person struggling. It feeds lies: You don't deserve help. You don't deserve love. You don't even deserve to try again. Over time, shame can make someone believe that the wreckage of their addiction is all they will ever be. That belief is lethal. It keeps people using when they desperately want to stop. It keeps families locked in patterns of silence that stifle healing.

The Tyranny of Shame

Shame is not passive, it is a tyrant. It rules by fear, controlling your choices, silencing your voice, and chaining you to the past. It doesn't just murmur, it commands: Don't tell anyone. Don't ask for help. Don't you dare believe you can change. It sabotages every fragile attempt at recovery. You skip the meeting, avoid the phone call, lie to the person you love, not because you don't care, but because shame has convinced you that the truth will destroy you.

For spiritual refugees, shame's tyranny can feel even heavier. When shame has been reinforced by religion, when you've been told that your addiction is not just a human struggle but a moral failure that disgusts God, it becomes almost unbearable. Shame tells you that even heaven has turned its back. It distorts grace into condemnation. It makes the God of love seem like a scorekeeper waiting to crush you.

Cultural and family systems often become accomplices to this tyranny. Families whisper, "We don't talk about things like that." Churches preach, "Good Christians don't struggle with addiction." Communities turn their backs, thinking humiliation will scare someone into changing. But humiliation never heals, it only hardens the walls of shame.

Shame is a dictator that wants to rule your future. It thrives in secrecy, feeding on your silence. It wants you to believe that no one could understand, that no one could still love you, that you are too far gone. But shame is a liar. The tyrant has no real power once it's exposed to light. Naming it, sharing your story, reaching for connection, all of these are acts of rebellion against its rule.

Speaking Healing Words Instead of Shame

Breaking shame's power begins with new words. Words that sound like:

"Me too."

"You are not your worst day."
"Your story isn't over."

Imagine Jenna walking into that basement meeting and hearing those words. The very thing she feared, judgment, was replaced with empathy. Someone's honest story became a lifeline. One compassionate phrase can stop shame in its tracks.

But shame doesn't only live in present failures, it lingers in memories. The past has a way of replaying like a cruel film strip, reminding you of every broken promise, every burned bridge, every hurtful word. The shame of facing one's past can feel unbearable. It insists, You can't move forward. You've already done too much damage. It tells you that healing is for other people, not for someone with your history. But moving forward is a must. The past may shape you, but it does not own your future. Recovery and healing demand that you stop letting yesterday's failures dictate tomorrow's possibilities.

Breaking shame's grip begins in the quiet moments when you choose a different story. Speaking words of truth is not about pretending the past didn't happen, it's about refusing to let it define what comes next. When you say, "I am more than what I've done," you are participating in something sacred. In recovery circles, many call it grace. Others call it love, light, or simply truth. Whatever name you give it, there is a spiritual power in words that reclaim identity. They carry a strength bigger than shame's accusations.

This isn't easy. Speaking new words might feel unnatural, even false, at first. But over time, the practice becomes a kind of quiet rebellion, a declaration that shame is not your ruler. Each time you affirm, "I am still worthy," or "My story is not over," you're breaking the spell of shame and inviting something greater, hope, grace, the sacred, to rewrite your story.

Families, too, can choose words that heal. Instead of, "You always ruin everything," they can say, "I love you enough to be honest. I won't enable you, but I'm here." Instead of, "You'll never change," they can try, "I believe change is possible, even if I can't see it yet." These are not magic fixes, but they create space for connection, the opposite of shame.

Hope and Reclaiming Identity

The tyranny of shame loses its power when identity is reclaimed. Addicts are not defined by their addiction. Families are not defined by their mistakes. You are not the sum of your worst decisions or your most painful failures.

Reclaiming identity can start small: saying to yourself, "I am more than my addiction." It can be sharing your story in a safe space, hearing another person say, "Me too," and realizing you're not alone. It can be practicing grounding exercises when shame threatens to spiral, taking a deep breath, touching something solid, naming five things you can see, to remind yourself you are still here, still worthy.

For spiritual refugees, this reclamation may mean separating the voice of shame from the voice of the sacred. Shame says, "You are worthless." The sacred says, "You are loved, even here." You do not need to step back into harmful spaces to find grace. Grace can find you in a basement meeting, a therapist's office, a late-night walk, or a quiet word spoken to a power you're not sure exists.

Shame will tell you to stay silent. But healing begins with a single, shaky word spoken aloud. Hope begins the moment you realize the tyrant is a fraud.

God Doesn't Do Shame

If your picture of God is a scowling judge keeping a ledger of your failures, hear this: that image is a distortion, not the divine. God does not wield shame as a weapon. The sacred does not delight in your humiliation or your collapse. The heart of God, call it Love, Grace, or Spirit, is not bent on condemnation but on restoration.

Throughout both the Hebrew Bible (Old Testament) and the New Testament, the story of God again and again reveals a God of love and compassion, a God who sees past failure and shame to the deeper truth of our humanity. The pages are full of moments where God chooses mercy over judgment, healing over punishment, and restoration over exclusion. These stories are not exceptions or rare footnotes; they are the heartbeat of the narrative. They remind us that shame was never meant to be the final word on anyone's life.

For many in recovery, especially spiritual refugees, this may feel impossible to believe. Years of religious shaming may have convinced you that heaven is disgusted with you. But what if God has never been the source of your shame? What if, even in your darkest moment, Love was sitting beside you in the wreckage, refusing to leave?

The journey of recovery is not about earning God's approval or groveling for worthiness, it's about discovering that you were never unworthy to begin with. The sacred meets you in the places you fear most: the late-night panic, the tear-streaked car seat, the trembling hand on a basement door handle. God does not keep score of your failures; God keeps reaching.

To heal, you may have to let the old image of a condemning God die and let a new image be born, a God whose eyes are soft with compassion, whose voice is steady with mercy, and whose hands are already extended toward you. In recovery, you are invited to know this God, not as a tyrant, but as a companion who walks with you toward freedom.

We Don't Do Shame

As the pastor and executive director of FREE Recovery Community, I can tell you: We Don't Do Shame. It's not just a catchy tagline, it's a battle cry. If you're reading this thinking you don't belong, that your past disqualifies you, that God is done with you, hear me: shame is lying to you.

In our community, we don't flinch at the mess. We lean in. We've sat with people who thought they were too far gone, who walked through our doors convinced everyone would judge them. And you know what happens? Nobody turns away. Nobody says, "You don't belong." We embrace the wreckage because wreckage is where grace does its best work.

But hear this clearly: We Don't Do Shame does not mean we don't do boundaries. It doesn't mean accountability is absent or that destructive behaviors are ignored. What it does mean is that love and compassion are always a better starting place than shame. Boundaries protect relationships, and accountability fosters growth, but they work best when they are grounded in dignity, not humiliation.

And here's the raw truth: belonging crushes shame. When you walk into a room and realize people see you, all of you, and don't turn away, something inside starts to shift. Belonging whispers a louder truth than shame ever could: you are worthy of love and belonging, no matter what's behind you. When belonging takes root, shame loses its grip. The old lies, that you're unworthy, unlovable, too broken, start to fade in the light of real connection.

This is where what we said about God comes alive, God doesn't do shame, and neither do we. If God isn't keeping score to crush you, why would we? Shame doesn't heal. Shame doesn't bring freedom. It never has, and it never will.

Reflection Questions for Chapter 4

Think of a time when shame silenced you or someone you love. How did it affect your ability to ask for or offer help?

In what ways have cultural, family, or religious systems used shame in your life? How has that shaped your understanding of yourself or of God?

What healing words or actions could you offer, to yourself or to someone else, that might interrupt shame's grip today?

How might reclaiming your identity apart from shame begin to change the way you move through recovery or support someone you love?

Chapter 5
Speaking Real, Not Preachy

The Moment Words Fell Flat

Kara sat at her friend's kitchen table, eyes red and raw from another night of worry. Her brother was back on the streets after promising to get clean. She hadn't eaten. She hadn't slept. When she finally reached out for help, someone from her old church offered a single line: "God won't give you more than you can handle." Kara nodded politely, but inside, something hardened. The words felt plastic. They didn't touch the ache in her chest or the panic in her stomach. She didn't need a slogan. She needed someone to sit in the wreckage with her.

This is what happens when we speak in clichés instead of truth. Platitudes might make us feel like we said something helpful, but for people in pain, they can deepen the wound. Addicts and their loved ones don't need polished sermons. They need real, messy, vulnerable words that say, "I see you, and I'm here."

Why Clichés and Religious Jargon Fail

People on the edge can spot fake or formulaic talk from a mile away. They've heard it all: "Everything happens for a reason." "God has a plan." "Just have more faith." To someone in the depths of addiction or loving someone who is, those words don't sound like comfort, they sound like dismissal. For spiritual refugees, they can sound like the very weapons that once drove them out of the church.

Spiritual refugees know the sting of words that reduced their pain to a slogan or implied that their suffering was their own fault. They've been told, outright or subtly, that if they just prayed harder, believed more, or behaved better, they wouldn't be in the mess they're in. When you've been burned by that kind of talk, even a whiff of it can slam the door on trust.

And this isn't just about avoiding churchy phrases to be trendy or "relevant." This is about following the way of Jesus. Jesus always spoke to real people, in real places, in a real moment of history, looking into their eyes and entering their suffering. He never used empty phrases to dodge someone's pain or fear to coerce them into obedience. Fear is not a good tactic, it never was, and yet it's been used by countless religious people as if scaring someone will heal their soul. It doesn't. It only deepens the wound.

To every pastor, counselor, sponsor, or friend trying to walk with people through addiction and recovery: this is the call to lay those phrases down. It might feel like ripping out part of your own spiritual vocabulary, because many of us were raised on those sayings. They're baked into sermons, devotionals, and coffee mug slogans. But if we want to speak to the ones who are drowning, we have to stop throwing them bumper stickers when what they need is a hand.

Yes, giving up clichés is hard. It means facing the awkwardness of silence when you don't have the perfect answer. It means admitting, "I don't know why this is happening" instead of papering over pain with a tidy platitude. But that honesty is holy. It's the language addicts, their loved ones, and spiritual refugees can actually trust.

Speaking real means acknowledging the chaos: "This is hard. It's unfair. It hurts like hell. And you're not alone." Those words cost more, they cost your vulnerability and your presence. But they're the ones that break through shame's walls and invite people to stay.

The Power of Vulnerability and Story

Stories change hearts. Vulnerability builds trust. If you've been through the fire, your scars will speak louder than any lecture. When you share honestly about your own broken moments, your doubts, your failures, the times you've been angry at God, you're saying, "Me too. I get it." That "me too" can save lives.

But let's be real: vulnerability is terrifying. If you've been burned before, if you've been met with judgment, silence, or condescending advice when you risked opening up, the thought of exposing your heart again feels impossible. You might be thinking, If I tell the truth about my pain, they'll reject me. They'll use it against me. They'll confirm every ugly thing I already suspect about myself.

Here's the truth no one told you: shame wants to keep you silent because silence keeps you stuck. The risk feels huge, but the payoff is freedom. Vulnerability isn't weakness, it's defiance. It's looking shame in the eye and saying, "You don't own me anymore." And when you go first, when you crack open your story even just a little, you give everyone around you permission to take off their masks too.

Religion has often discouraged vulnerability, teaching people to hide their doubts and polish their stories until they shine. But if we want authentic faith spaces where real transformation happens, we must lean into vulnerability. And here's where it gets personal: leaders, I know the fear you feel. You've been told to keep it together, to project strength, to never let the cracks show. You're afraid that if you expose your struggles, people will lose respect or walk away. That fear is real, it's heavy, and it's valid.

But here's the deeper truth: people don't need perfect leaders. They need honest ones. When you step into that fear and show up as a whole, imperfect human, you give your community the courage to do the same. Your willingness to be vulnerable says, "It's safe here. You don't have to hide." That's how walls crumble. That's how authentic faith is born, not through polished performances, but through shared humanity.

I know this from experience. When I got sober in 2013, I wasn't just another guy fighting addiction, I was a pastor. I was the drunk pastor, and the shame of that nearly crushed me. For the first three years of my recovery, I stayed silent, hoping and praying no one would ever find out that behind the sermons and the Sunday smiles, I was an alcoholic. I was suffocating under the weight of my own hypocrisy, terrified that if people knew the truth, it would all come crashing down.

Three years in, with the help of my sponsor and trusted mentors, I finally broke the silence. On a Sunday morning, at all three worship services, I stood trembling, voice shaking, and shared my story. I was convinced some people would walk out, whisper behind my back, or never look at me the same again.

But something else happened. I was met with grace. I was met with compassion. And in that sacred moment, something cracked open, not just in me, but in the room. People came forward with their own stories. They whispered their broken places. They trusted me with their pain. I realized how many were quietly drowning, desperate for someone to go first.

That morning changed everything. It was one of the moments that gave birth to FREE Recovery Community, the space my wife, Tami, and I later built for addicts, loved ones of addicts, and spiritual refugees. If you're reading this and you're terrified to let anyone see behind your mask, hear me: your story has power. Someone else's healing might begin with your honesty. Don't let shame keep you silent another day. The world doesn't need your perfection, it needs your truth.

Real Talk for Real Addicts

Let's be honest: for many addicts and spiritual refugees, the way the church has traditionally spoken, the insider language, the polished slogans, the heavy religious symbols, hasn't felt like love. It's often felt like a locked door. It's not that those words or symbols are evil or worthless. They can carry deep beauty and meaning. But they can never be the first thing. They cannot be the opening handshake.

Faith leaders, this part is for you. If the cross on the wall, the insider phrases, or the "Christianese" jargon are keeping wounded people from even stepping through the doorway, you need the courage to set them aside. People always come before traditions. Jesus modeled this over and over. He chose the person over the ritual, the relationship over the rule. Choosing the suffering over the symbol is not betrayal, it's discipleship.

Jesus didn't start conversations with doctrinal statements or polished prayers. He knelt in the dirt with a woman caught in shame. He ate dinner with people the religious establishment avoided. He told stories about seeds and storms, fathers and lost sons, because real people in real pain needed words that met them on the ground.

Traditions can be beautiful. Rituals can heal. But they are never the doorway to grace for someone who already feels unworthy or unwelcome. If religious symbols and insider talk feel like a barrier, then have the guts to get rid of them, or at least move them out of the way, until love has done its work.

Faith leaders searching for a new way: speak the language of the street, the recovery circle, and the broken heart. Don't ask people to decode your world before they can be welcomed. Build the bridge. Meet them where they are. That's not watering down the gospel, that's following Jesus.

Practical Tools for Communicating Realness

Listen more than you talk. Sometimes the holiest thing you can do is shut up and stay present. Let the silence speak louder than advice.

Ask honest, open questions. Instead of, "Why can't you just stop?" try, "What does the struggle feel like today?"

Choose empathy over persuasion. You're not trying to win a debate, you're trying to build a bridge.

Honor pain without fixing it. Resist the urge to tie a neat bow on someone's suffering. It's okay to say, "I don't know what to say, but I'm here."

Speak from your scars, not your pedestal. Authenticity is magnetic. Pretending you've got it all together creates distance.

When Real Words Heal

Imagine Kara again, but this time, instead of hearing "God won't give you more than you can handle," she hears: "This is brutal. I can see how exhausted you are. You don't have to hold this alone." That simple, real response doesn't fix everything. But it gives her a breath of relief. It tells her she's not invisible. It tells her she's worth listening to.

Speaking real is not about perfect phrasing. It's about presence. It's about showing up with honesty, humility, and a willingness to stand in the mess. For addicts, their loved ones, and spiritual refugees, those words can be a lifeline, proof that connection is still possible, even in the wreckage.

Reflection Questions for Chapter 5

Recall a time when someone's words felt hollow or hurtful in a hard moment. What made them miss the mark?

Think of a time when someone spoke to you with honesty and vulnerability. How did it affect you?

What clichés or phrases do you need to unlearn so you can speak more authentically to those in pain?

How might your own scars or struggles become part of the way you communicate hope without preaching?

Chapter 6
Teaching Spiritual Wisdom Without Religious Baggage

The Weight of Religious Baggage

For many people, especially spiritual refugees and those scarred by addiction, religion has been less a source of comfort and more a source of pain. Maybe it was the preacher who thundered judgment instead of offering grace. Maybe it was the youth leader who told you your questions were rebellion instead of curiosity. Maybe it was the church that turned its back when addiction, divorce, or depression got too messy for their image. Perhaps it was the whispered conversations about who you loved, or the unspoken rules about which skin color, income level, or theology was really acceptable.

This kind of exclusion, naming who is "in" and who is "out," has wounded countless people. When leaders claim that God's love is only for the insiders, it doesn't just hurt those pushed out. It poisons everyone. It plants the fear: "If they're not in, how can I be sure I am?" That kind of thinking breeds anxiety, shame, and division. It is not the heart of God.

The weight of this baggage can be crushing. It presses down like a stone on your chest, making every breath feel heavy. It distorts the face of God until God looks more like a gatekeeper than a source of grace. For many, even the language of faith has become a trigger, a reminder of rejection and control.

But here's the truth: the whole thing has to be more inclusive if it's going to resemble the God revealed in love. God doesn't fit in the boxes we've built. Trying to contain God in rigid systems or small circles of approval doesn't work. Addicts and the loved ones of addicts figured this out long ago. To climb out of the hole, to survive, they had to imagine a God far bigger, kinder, and freer than the one they were handed. They had to believe in a Love that could reach them in the gutter or in the pit of despair, a Love that wasn't limited to clean hands and polished reputations.

If that's you, if you've been told you don't belong, hear this: your pain is real, and you are not alone. Walking away from harmful religion doesn't mean walking away from God. It means seeking the God who is already seeking you. The Divine is not threatened by your doubts, your anger, your brokenness, or your hope for something truer. God is bigger, wider, and wilder than the exclusionary thinking that hurt you. And that bigger Love is already reaching for you.

For spiritual refugees, this matters: you're not rejecting the sacred just because you've rejected what hurt you. And for leaders, this is your reminder: a healthy image of God is one of love and compassion, not condemnation. The God who meets people in their brokenness is not fragile or threatened by your questions.

If you're a faith leader, you need to know this: people are walking into your spaces carrying wounds you can't always see. Your favorite phrases, rituals, or symbols might feel safe to you but may reopen old scars for someone else. Wisdom begins with seeing their pain before defending your traditions.

Unearthing Wisdom Beyond Walls

Spiritual wisdom doesn't live only in pulpits or holy books. It pulses through the rhythms of everyday life, in the bass-line of a song that breaks you open, in the sunrise that catches you off guard, in the trembling voice of someone in a recovery circle saying, "I almost didn't make it here tonight." Wisdom can be found in poetry, laughter around a dinner table, the wind across your face during a walk, or the tearful "me too" from someone who has been where you are.

Scripture, whether in the Hebrew Bible (Old Testament) or the New Testament, is a rich well of wisdom. It gives us stories of failure and redemption, of exiles finding home, of outcasts being seen, and of broken people being restored. It offers deep truths about love, justice, mercy, and grace. But it is not our only well. The sacred is not confined to the pages of a single book. God's wisdom shows up in the voice of a sponsor, in the honesty of a friend, in recovery slogans, in art and nature, and in the places religion sometimes overlooks.

Faith leaders, this is where you must pause and ask yourself: Who are you really trying to reach? Is your mission to impress other church people, or is it to stand with the suffering, the broken, the cast out, and the marginalized? If it's the latter, and it should be, then some of your cherished traditions and "churchy" ways might need to go. If a ritual, phrase, or symbol makes insiders comfortable but pushes outsiders away, it is sabotaging the very mission you claim to serve.

If it kills the mission, kill the tradition. Jesus did this constantly. He healed on the Sabbath even when the religious gatekeepers bristled, and he welcomed those others dismissed as unclean. He showed us that God's love is too urgent and too wild to be bound by rules that protect the powerful but ignore the hurting. When the mission is to reach the desperate and the forgotten, the comfort of insiders cannot be the priority.

For leaders, this means learning to dance with multiple sources of wisdom and letting God lead you beyond your comfort zone. Scripture is vital, but it is not the only teacher. God is not limited to your tradition, your translation, or your preferred theology. God is big enough to be present in the trembling story of an addict, the lyrics of a song on the radio, or the fragile hope you feel standing under a star-filled sky.

This can be unsettling for those of us who were trained to guard the boundaries of "orthodox" answers. But the Spirit moves where it will, refusing to be boxed in by our systems. To teach spiritual wisdom without religious baggage, you have to be willing to step outside the familiar walls and trust that God will meet you there. That trust doesn't dilute scripture, it honors it. The same scriptures that tell of prophets hearing God in whispers and shepherds seeing angels also remind us that the Divine cannot be contained. God's fingerprints are everywhere, waiting to be noticed.

Practices That Don't Hurt

Spiritual practices don't have to be complicated or wrapped in dogma. They can be simple, raw, and accessible:

Breathing: Take three slow, deliberate breaths. Notice you're alive.

Gratitude lists: Write down three things you're grateful for, even if one of them is simply, "I made it through today."

Story circles: Share one moment from your week that stirred something in you. Listen without fixing, without preaching.

Nature walks: Step outside. Let the wind on your skin remind you that you're part of something bigger.

Prayer and meditation: Spend a few quiet moments each day centering yourself. This doesn't have to be formal or scripted. It can be as simple as speaking honestly to God or sitting in silence to listen.

Reading sacred texts: Explore scripture or other writings that carry wisdom and hope. Scripture remains an important source, but it can be approached with fresh eyes. Read not as a weapon, but as a guide that points to grace.

These practices don't demand you recite creeds or sign statements of belief. They invite you to show up as you are. For spiritual refugees, these can be gentle doorways into connection without fear of judgment. And for many, this is where God meets them again, not in shame or control, but in tenderness and presence.

Humility, Curiosity, and Questions

Teaching wisdom without baggage requires humility. It requires you to admit you don't have all the answers. That's hard, especially for leaders who were trained to be certain, to defend every doctrine, to never say "I don't know." But questions are not a threat to faith, they're a pathway to it. Questions open doors that certainty keeps shut. They invite dialogue, exploration, and growth. Far from disqualifying you, your honest questions can establish a deeper, more resilient spiritual path.

Doubt isn't the enemy of faith; indifference is. Doubt means you care enough to wrestle with the big stuff. In fact, doubt often has a way of deepening faith, stripping away shallow clichés and forcing us to encounter the sacred in a more honest way. For Jesus, doubt was never a problem. In Matthew's gospel, when the disciples stood on the mountain with Jesus after the resurrection, it says some worshiped and some doubted. Jesus didn't rebuke the doubters. He didn't send them away. He stood with them, gave them a mission, and trusted them to carry hope into the world, even with their questions.

Curiosity is powerful. Ask, "What gives you hope right now?" or "What's been the hardest part of today?" or even "Where do you feel most alive?" These aren't tests of orthodoxy. They're invitations into deeper connection. Wisdom grows in the space where people feel safe to explore, doubt, and wonder.

Leaders, the world doesn't need more polished speeches. It needs guides who are willing to learn alongside the brokenhearted. Teach by asking, by listening, by modeling wonder. Show that faith can be a journey, not a sales pitch. God is not threatened by questions, God meets people in them.

A Call to Leaders
People Over Systems

This is where it gets uncomfortable. If your traditions, rituals, or symbols are keeping wounded people from walking through the door, you have a choice: protect the system or protect the people. Jesus chose people every time. He healed on the Sabbath even when the rule-keepers protested. He touched lepers. He welcomed outsiders. He broke religious expectations to love the unloved.

But I also want to affirm you, the leader, the sponsor, the parent, the friend, who is struggling to find a new way of being. It isn't easy to set aside what you've always known. It isn't easy to rethink the phrases, practices, and postures you were handed. It's hard work to unlearn old habits and risk vulnerability with people who carry deep scars. And yet, every time you choose to love over fear, to listen instead of preach, to show up instead of turn away, you are stepping into sacred ground.

To those of you willing to try: you are already part of the transformation. You are choosing the path Jesus modeled, the path where relationships matter more than rules, where connection is valued above control, and where grace outweighs judgment. You are building a new kind of community where addicts, their loved ones, and spiritual refugees can breathe again.

But hear this, too: we cannot wait for perfect conditions or for someone else to go first. The wounds are too deep, the stakes too high. People are dying in silence, believing they are beyond reach. They need us now. They need your courage, your humanity, your willingness to step into the mess.

So here is the plea: Let love guide you, even when it costs you comfort. Let compassion outrun your fear of getting it wrong. Dare to dismantle the barriers that keep people out. Dare to create spaces where scars are honored, where doubts are welcome, and where God's grace is bigger than anyone imagined. Choose people over systems, every single time.

Faith leaders, addicts, families, and spiritual refugees alike: rejecting harmful religion doesn't mean rejecting God. It means clearing away what is toxic so that something true can live. God is not done with you. God's wisdom is waiting, in the stories you tell, in the breath you take, in the quiet spaces where love whispers, "You're not alone."

Reflection Questions for Chapter 6

When you think about the religious baggage you may carry, what specific memories, messages, or experiences feel the heaviest? How have they shaped your image of God or community?

Where outside of traditional religious spaces (nature, music, recovery groups, conversations with friends) have you experienced something sacred or life-giving? How did that moment invite you to imagine God differently?

What traditions, phrases, or "churchy" habits might you need to let go of (either personally or within your community) in order to reach the suffering, the broken, and the marginalized more effectively?

Which spiritual practices (breathing, prayer, meditation, reading sacred texts, gratitude lists, story circles) feel most accessible to you right now? How could one of these help you reconnect with hope or invite others into healing this week?

Chapter 7
Listening as a Radical Act

The Silence That Saves

It was late on a Thursday night when Jason sat alone in his car outside a recovery meeting. His hands trembled on the steering wheel, knuckles white against the leather. In his mind, he had rehearsed a dozen versions of what he might say if he walked inside. Each one was a carefully crafted half-truth designed to make him look better, less desperate. He imagined introducing himself in a way that would soften the edges of his pain, mentioning the stress at work, the rough patch in his marriage, the bad luck that led him here. Anything but the raw reality: that his drinking had wrecked relationships, cost him jobs, and left him staring at the ceiling most nights, wondering if life was still worth trying.

Jason had been taught all his life to keep up appearances. Growing up in a small church community, weakness wasn't something you showed. You smiled, said you were "fine," and kept your mess behind closed doors. The polished explanations weren't just about pride; they were armor. They protected him from judgment, from pity, and from the terrifying possibility that if people really knew him, they'd walk away.

As he sat there, rehearsing his lines, shame pressed on him like a weight. The idea of admitting the truth (that he was drowning) felt unbearable. Then a man from the meeting noticed him and quietly approached. He didn't ask for Jason's story or offer advice. He leaned against the hood of Jason's car and said softly, "You don't have to do this alone." They stood there in the quiet, no speeches, no demands. For the first time in months, Jason felt seen without needing to perform.

Listening, and sometimes even silent listening, can pull a person back from the edge. In a world overflowing with noise and opinions, true listening is a quiet rebellion. It says: Your story matters. You matter. And this kind of listening is not just kind; it is urgent. Without it, people stay trapped in hopelessness and despair. Some are so crushed by silence and shame that they take their own lives. We stand in solidarity with them when we choose to listen without fixing or preaching. Listening is the act that comes first, the simple but sacred doorway to hope.

Why Listening Feels So Hard

Listening sounds simple, but it costs something. It means slowing down when everything in our culture shouts, "Hurry!" It means sitting with discomfort when everything in us wants to fix, explain, or move on. For loved ones of addicts, listening can feel like weakness: "If I don't say something, will they think I approve?" For spiritual refugees, even stepping into a conversation where someone claims to "know what's best" can reopen wounds.

The truth is, listening threatens our illusion of control. Advice makes us feel useful. Fixing gives us the sense that we're in charge. But presence (just being there) can feel terrifying because it forces us to face how powerless we sometimes are. Listening asks us to stand in the middle of someone's pain without reaching for easy answers.

Jesus understood this. He listened to people others ignored. He stopped for a woman who touched His robe, letting her tell the whole truth while everyone else urged Him to move on. He knelt in the dust while an angry crowd demanded judgment, waiting for the woman accused of adultery to find her voice instead of silencing her with condemnation. He shared meals with tax collectors and sinners, hearing their stories without shaming them into silence. He let blind men call out to Him over the noise of the crowd, asking, "What do you want me to do for you?" as if their voices and desires mattered more than the expectations of the religious elite.

This is the power of listening: it restores dignity. It tells people who have been shamed, dismissed, or overlooked that they are seen and valued. Jesus' listening was not passive; it was a radical act that healed hearts before any miracle touched their bodies. And it still heals today when we choose to listen like that.

Listening as Love in Action

Listening is not passive. It is an act of love. Recovery wisdom says, "We're heard into healing." To truly listen is to say: You don't have to edit yourself for me. You don't have to dress up your pain to make it palatable.

For addicts and spiritual refugees, who have often been lectured, judged, or dismissed, listening is proof that their humanity is intact. It's a declaration: "Your worth isn't tied to your performance. I will hold space for you exactly as you are."

But this applies just as much to the loved ones of addicts. They carry their own silent wounds, years of sleepless nights, second-guessing every decision, and bracing themselves for the next crisis. Too often, families feel invisible. They are told to "just detach" or "stay strong" without anyone pausing to hear their heartbreak. Listening to them is an act of compassion that says: Your pain matters too. Your fear, your anger, your exhaustion are real, and they deserve a safe place to land.

When families and friends are given space to tell their truth without judgment, shame loses some of its grip on them as well. It allows them to breathe, to grieve, and to begin healing their own hearts, not just for the sake of the addict they love, but for themselves. Listening restores dignity on both sides of addiction's wreckage.

Listening Without Agenda

Many of us are guilty of listening with an agenda. We wait for the pause in someone's story so we can insert advice, a Scripture verse, or a "Have you tried…?" But radical listening doesn't manipulate or steer. It doesn't sit in judgment or subtly try to fix. It invites the other person to unfold without fear of correction.

Reflective listening can help: repeating back what you hear ("It sounds like you're feeling exhausted and afraid") or validating their experience ("That sounds brutal; I can see why you're overwhelmed"). These simple phrases are lifelines for people who've been dismissed or shamed.

Presence Over Perfection

You don't need perfect words to make a difference. "I'm here" is often enough. Presence communicates what advice never can: that the person's pain is not too heavy to bear and their story is not too messy to be heard.

But perfectionism can get in the way. Too often, we hold back from showing up because we're afraid of saying the wrong thing or not knowing the "right" prayer or advice. We delay reaching out, waiting until we're fully prepared. Yet that delay can leave someone feeling even more abandoned. Our obsession with doing it "right" can cause real harm.

The truth is, God never needed our perfection anyway. Throughout the gospels, Jesus never demanded perfect words or perfect behavior before offering love. He simply showed up for people where they were at a well, on a roadside, in a tax collector's home and everywhere. In the same way, addicts, their loved ones, and spiritual refugees don't need you to be flawless. They need your presence. They need to know that even in your awkwardness, your uncertainty, and your trembling voice, you will sit with them. Showing up imperfectly is still showing up. Perfectionism builds walls. Presence tears them down.

When Words Are Needed

Listening doesn't mean silence forever. Sometimes, after trust is built, gentle words can bring hope. But timing matters. Speaking too soon can shut a person down or make them feel judged. The first step is to listen long enough that the other person feels seen, not evaluated.

When the time is right, your words don't have to be profound. They don't have to fix the situation or offer an airtight solution. Often, the most healing words are simple and honest: "I don't have all the answers, but I'm with you." Or, "This sounds unbearable, and I see your strength in showing up today." These phrases remind the other person that they're not alone and that their story isn't too big for love to hold.

Sometimes, when someone is spiraling, a quiet reminder of hope, spoken without pressure, can help them take the next breath. But let your words be slow, soft, and offered from humility. Speak only after you've earned the right to be heard. Presence first. Words second. In this way, your voice becomes a bridge, not a barrier.

Barriers to Radical Listening

Several barriers can keep us from truly listening:

Pride: Believing you already know what's best.

Fear: Worrying you'll hear something painful or be drawn into chaos.

Distraction: Letting busyness and noise crowd out presence.

Breaking these barriers takes humility and courage. It means recognizing that listening is not about control, but about connection.

The Spiritual Dimension of Listening

Listening mirrors the way God meets us, not with condemnation, but with presence. Throughout scripture, God listens: to the cries of the oppressed, to Hannah's silent prayer, to Jesus weeping in a garden. For spiritual refugees, it is vital to remember that God is not the voice of shaming lectures. God is the quiet Presence that hears your groaning even when you cannot form words.

Listening can also be a spiritual discipline for the listener. When you sit with someone else's pain without flinching, you begin to see God's image in them… and in yourself. You learn to trust that grace can hold stories too heavy for you to carry alone.

A Call to the Community

Communities of healing are built on radical listening. But let's be honest, this is not easy work. Creating a culture of listening requires time, humility, and a willingness to feel uncomfortable. It's far simpler to stick with surface-level conversations or retreat into cliques of people who think, talk, and live like us. But if we are serious about creating spaces where addicts, their loved ones, and spiritual refugees can breathe again, we must commit to the hard, holy work of listening.

In your community, create intentional moments where stories can be shared and truly heard. Practice using phrases like, "Tell me more," or "That sounds really heavy; thank you for trusting us with that." Make it explicit: the goal is not to fix, rescue, or debate, but to bear witness. Establish simple ground rules: confidentiality, no interrupting, no unsolicited advice, and no judgment. These boundaries allow people who have been silenced or shamed elsewhere to speak honestly.

At FREE Recovery Community, our services are on Saturday nights. After my sermon, we always invite a guest storyteller to share some of their experience, strength, and hope around the evening's topic. In that space, they speak freely, without fear of judgment or condemnation. Their story is not edited or sanitized. They are sharing hope, and we as the community get to listen. It is a living, practical example of radical listening, and the responsibility rests on all of us, not just one individual. The power is in the collective willingness to hear, to hold space, and to honor someone's truth.

Equip your community with listening tools. Teach reflective listening techniques: repeat or paraphrase what someone said so they feel understood. Encourage active listening. Turn off phones, make eye contact, and resist the urge to craft a response while someone is still speaking. Practice silence. Sometimes the most powerful gift is to sit quietly, letting the weight of someone's story settle in the room without rushing to fill it.

Affirm the reality that this work is exhausting at times. Hearing hard stories can stir up your own pain, trigger your fears, or leave you feeling helpless. That's normal. Listening is not about having infinite strength; it's about showing up with the strength you have and trusting that grace fills in the gaps. Take care of yourself as you care for others: debrief with trusted friends or mentors, step back when needed, and ground yourself with your own practices of prayer, meditation, or reflection.

Radical listening disrupts cycles of shame. It builds bridges between people who thought they had nothing in common. It reminds those drowning in despair that they are not invisible.

To the one reading this who feels overwhelmed by the task: your effort matters. Even if you're not sure you're doing it "right," your willingness to listen can change someone's life. The addict at the edge, the loved one holding on by a thread, the spiritual refugee wondering if any faith community could ever be safe again, need communities that will stand with them. Communities where silence is broken by compassionate ears. Communities that choose presence over perfection.

This work is not easy. It will stretch your patience, your heart, and your ego. But it is necessary work. It is the work of grace. And every time you lean in to hear a story, you create a sacred space where hope can breathe again.

Reflection Questions for Chapter 7

When was the last time someone truly listened to you without interrupting, fixing, or judging? How did it affect you?

What fears or habits keep you from listening deeply to others, especially those in pain?

Think about a loved one or community member affected by addiction. How might radical listening change your relationship with them?

How could you or your community intentionally create safe spaces where people can tell their stories without fear of shame or exclusion?

Chapter 8
Helping the Wrecked Without Playing Savior

The Breaking Point
A Brother-to-Brother Confrontation

The shouting started before Eli even closed the front door. Mark's voice cracked under the weight of anger and exhaustion: "You lied to me again, Eli. I covered your rent again and you said you were clean." His fists clenched at his sides, not in threat but in a desperate attempt to keep himself from breaking apart. Eli stood there, shoulders sagging, the smell of stale liquor trailing in behind him.

"This isn't what you think," Eli muttered, eyes fixed on the floorboards. But Mark wasn't buying it. He was tired of the stories, the half-truths. Tired of watching his brother spiral while their family drained savings accounts and pawned memories just to keep him afloat. Tired of the whispered arguments with their parents about whether to cut Eli off. The bills were piling up. The trust was in pieces. And worst of all, the faith that had once anchored their family now felt like another casualty.

"Do you even realize what you're doing to us?" Mark's voice rose, then cracked into something softer, half rage, half heartbreak. "Dad's working extra shifts. Mom barely speaks. And me? I'm standing here wondering if I should hate you or hug you." The silence that followed was suffocating. Eli finally looked up, his own anger flickering before dissolving into something far more painful: shame.

In that moment, there were no perfect words. No tidy solutions. Just two brothers caught in the wreckage of addiction, one drowning in it, the other gasping for air nearby.

Naming the Wreckage Families Carry

Families living with addiction walk through invisible minefields. Every day feels like bracing for the next explosion. Financial strain becomes a constant companion, mortgages are missed, savings accounts vanish, and vacations are quietly canceled. Broken trust hangs in the air like smoke that won't clear. Anger at God simmers alongside anger at each other, and shame shadows every family gathering. It's not just the addict who feels ashamed, it's the whole family. Shame whispers that you must have done something wrong, that people are watching, that you're alone in this.

To the brother, sister, parent, or spouse reading this: your exhaustion is real. Your hurt is valid. You've been living in a storm that doesn't let up, and you're tired of pretending everything is fine. You are not weak for feeling broken, you're human.

Why Communication Often Breaks Down

When fear and exhaustion take over, communication can become another casualty. Sometimes we speak from panic: words come out sharp, barbed, or desperate. Other times, we retreat into silence, thinking it's safer not to say anything at all. Anger becomes a shield. Ultimatums become weapons. Conversations are avoided because everyone's too scared to ignite another fight.

In families, these patterns are common:

Conversations that start with love but spiral into accusations.

Late-night texts full of blame and regret.

The silent treatment, which feels safer than risking more hurt.

Half-hearted small talk, because speaking the real pain feels impossible.

If you recognize yourself in these patterns, you're not alone. None of us communicate perfectly when the stakes feel life-and-death. The good news: there's another way.

Speaking Truth Without Shame or Blame

Speaking truth to someone you love is hard, especially when addiction has wrecked trust. But shaming or blaming rarely brings healing. Shame corners people. It drives them deeper into isolation, and isolation feeds addiction. Blame might feel justified, but it builds walls instead of bridges.

The blame game is a never-ending cycle that can trap everyone involved. When blame starts flying, it does not just sting, it spirals. It turns every conversation into a battlefield where no one wins. Blame can make the person using feel hunted, so they retreat or lash out. It can make family members feel righteous for a moment but emptier afterward. It is a dangerous spiral because it keeps everyone locked in their roles: the accuser and the accused, the rescuer and the villain.

Worse, blame invites us to play the role of the victim. It whispers that all the power and responsibility lie somewhere else, that if only the other person changed, everything would be fixed. But staying in victim mode never gets anyone anywhere. It does not heal wounds or rebuild trust. It keeps everyone stuck.

Honest communication begins with humility and compassion. Use "I" statements to speak from your heart instead of accusing:

"I'm scared for you" instead of "You're destroying us."

"I feel hurt when you lie" instead of "You're a liar."

Avoid character attacks. Focus on behavior and its impact. Anchor your words in love, not control. Remind yourself: your goal is connection, not victory in an argument.

And remember, speaking truth does not mean excusing destructive behavior. You can name the harm without condemning the person. You can say, "This isn't okay," while still saying, "I love you."

Boundaries That Hold Love

Boundaries are not betrayals, they are lifelines. They are the fences that keep love safe. In families wrecked by addiction, boundaries can feel cruel. Guilt whispers that setting a limit is abandonment. But the truth is, boundaries are the opposite of giving up, they're what make it possible to stay.

Boundaries might sound like:

"I can't give you money, but I'll take you to dinner."

"I can't let you stay here if you're high, but I'll pick you up tomorrow morning."

"I love you, but I won't lie for you anymore."

These words don't come easy. Your voice might shake. Your heart might break. That's normal. Boundaries are difficult because love is deep. But boundaries keep relationships from collapsing completely under the weight of chaos. They are acts of courage and compassion, holding space for love while refusing to enable harm.

Listening Even When It Hurts

Listening to a loved one caught in addiction can feel unbearable. You might hear denial, anger, or blame turned back on you. You may feel every word as a fresh wound. But listening does not equal agreement or approval. Listening is about bearing witness. It's about saying, "I see your pain, even when it's messy."

Staying grounded can help:

Take a deep breath before responding.

If needed, step away for a moment to collect yourself.

Afterward, lean on your own support, friends, mentors, or trusted community members who can hold your feelings without judgment.

Listening even when it hurts is not about letting someone walk all over you, it's about creating space where shame loses its grip.

The Spiritual Dimension of Talking Through Wreckage

When families are torn apart by addiction, anger at God is common. You may have prayed a thousand prayers and still watched the bottom fall out. You may have felt abandoned or betrayed by the faith you once trusted. Spiritual refugees often carry scars from churches that responded with platitudes or condemnation instead of compassion.

But God is not the voice of shame or the author of abandonment. God is present in the wreckage, quiet, patient, and strong enough to hold your anger. Jesus himself sat with the grieving, the doubting, and the outcasts without demanding polished faith. When you speak truth or sit in silence with your loved one, you mirror that divine presence. You do not need to defend God or the church. You are not called to fix someone else's soul. You are called to love, even in the mess.

Talking through wreckage is a spiritual act because it says, "I will not let shame or despair have the last word." It creates a small sanctuary right where you are.

Practical Tools for Hard Conversations

Hard conversations are rarely neat, but you can prepare yourself:

Prepare your own heart first. Take time to breathe, pray, meditate, or journal before approaching a loved one. Center yourself so fear and anger don't steer the conversation.

Pick your moment wisely. Avoid starting deep conversations in the middle of a crisis or a fight. Wait until emotions have cooled enough for real dialogue.

Use grounding phrases. Simple, clear language works best:

"I love you too much to stay silent."

"I'm here, but I can't rescue you."

"I trust you to take the next step."

Have support ready. After the conversation, debrief with a trusted friend or mentor. Let someone hold space for your emotions. You are not meant to carry this alone.

A Word to the One Holding On by a Thread

If you are reading this and feel like you are at the end of yourself, if the bills are past due, if the trust is shattered, if you are angry at God and angry at everyone else, hear this: your pain is real, and your love still matters. You are not weak because you are tired. You are tired because you have been fighting a battle bigger than you.

To the one pacing the floor at 3 a.m., replaying every conversation, wondering if you missed some magic phrase that could have saved them…you didn't. To the one hiding the empty bottles, covering the lies, or keeping secrets to protect a family image; you are not alone, and you are not invisible. To the one who has prayed until your knees ached, screamed into a pillow, or whispered to the ceiling, "God, where are You?", your cries have been heard.

You are carrying a weight no one was ever meant to carry alone. Addiction is a thief, and it has been stealing from you, too. It has stolen your sleep, your trust, your laughter, and maybe even your faith. It has tried to convince you that you are powerless and abandoned. But hear this clearly: you are not powerless, and you are not abandoned.

It is okay to fall apart. It is okay to scream, cry, and question everything. But do not believe the lie that you are out of options. Even here, in the wreckage, hope is still alive. It may not look polished or pretty, but it is breathing. It is the friend who texts you just when you are about to give up. It is the community that will hold you even when you can't hold yourself. It is the whisper of grace reminding you that this is not the end of the story.

And know this: God identifies with your suffering. In Luke's gospel, Jesus tells the story of a father who must have stood at the edge of the road every single day, scanning the horizon for his lost son. That father knew what it was like to wait with a broken heart, to feel the ache of absence, to love without guarantees. God is that Father. God knows what it is to wait, to hope, to grieve, and to love relentlessly. When you feel invisible and abandoned, remember: the God who waits on the road understands your tears and your longing. God is not distant from your pain…God is standing beside you in it.

You are not required to save your loved one. You cannot fix them by loving harder or sacrificing more. That burden will crush you. What you can do is stay tethered to love, to truth, and to people who will hold your hand when you're too tired to stand. Take the next small step: call a friend, go to a meeting, pray an unpolished prayer, or just breathe. You are not alone, and you do not have to fight this battle by yourself.

Closing Vision
A Community Where No One Is Alone

Imagine a community where conversations about addiction are not whispered but welcomed. Where family members can cry, shout, or confess without fear of condemnation. Where the addict is not reduced to their worst choices and the family is not reduced to blame. Where people believe in a God bigger than their pain, one who does not shame, but heals.

This is what we are building together. Not perfection. Not quick fixes. But sacred, messy spaces where love speaks louder than shame and listening carries the weight of grace. Talking with loved ones who are wrecked is not a strategy, it's an act of solidarity. It's saying, "Even here, in the rubble, we will find ways to speak life."

At FREE Recovery Community, this is why we all gather together, addicts, loved ones of addicts, and spiritual refugees, because we're all in this together. We listen, we weep, we celebrate, and we remind each other of hope. Our mission is to break the silence of addiction while creating space for healing, recovery, and spiritual connection. This mission matters deeply in a world where so many people feel alone, convinced they're battling their demons in isolation. At FREE, we remind each other that we never have to do it alone. We can break the silence together, and we don't do shame. This kind of community doesn't just happen, it is built intentionally, brick by brick, story by story, and act of grace by act of grace. It is the hard, holy work of creating a place where no one has to face the wreckage alone.

Reflection Questions for Chapter 8

When have your words, spoken in fear or anger, caused unintended harm in a hard conversation? How might you approach that conversation differently today?

What boundaries feel both necessary and terrifying for you to hold with someone you love?

How could shifting from blame to compassionate truth-telling create space for healing in one of your relationships?

Who in your community can hold space for you after you've had a difficult conversation? How might you invite them in?

Chapter 9
The Language of Hope Without the BS

My Story
Hope in the Ruins

It was Monday morning, January 7, 2013. I was passed out on the couch again. My head throbbed, my mouth was dry, and I could hear my wife, Tami, getting ready for work upstairs. I popped up off the couch, trying to make it look like I had my life together, even though I was hungover and broken. As I walked toward the staircase, I saw her at the top, standing still, holding another empty vodka bottle I had hidden. I had bottles stashed all over the house, thinking I was clever.

Tami's tears streamed down her face as she looked at me and said, "Ryan, what are we gonna do?" And for some reason, in that exact moment, I heard her. Really heard her. It was like the game was up. I heard the "we" in her question and knew I wasn't alone. That morning was the breaking point and the beginning. It was the day I threw myself into a 12-step program of recovery. I haven't picked up a drink since.

Tami and I didn't just magically recover that day. We stayed together, but it took brutal honesty, therapy, late-night tears, and a lot of grace. We each had to heal, separately and side by side. And today, what we have is a marriage and a family that's not perfect, but it's beautiful and real. Out of the wreckage came redemption. We get to walk this road of recovery together now, shoulder to shoulder with others who understand this fight. That is a miracle we never take for granted, and it's proof that even in the ruins, hope can rise.

That moment wasn't glamorous or cinematic. There was no perfect music swell, no quick fix, no lightning bolt of certainty. It was raw. It was ugly. And it was real. It's proof that hope doesn't arrive in shiny packaging. Sometimes hope comes wearing yesterday's clothes, reeking of vodka, staring at you from the top of the stairs with tears in her eyes.

Why Cheap Positivity Fails

People love to offer quick fixes because it makes the chaos feel controllable. "Everything happens for a reason." "God doesn't give you more than you can handle." "Just think positive." Maybe you've heard those lines. Maybe you've said them. But let's be honest: when your world is burning down, those words can sting. They don't heal. They dismiss. They make the suffering person feel unseen.

Cheap positivity isn't hope, it's denial in a pretty package. It's a way to avoid entering the pain. And for those who've been hurt by religious platitudes, those words don't just fall flat, they reopen wounds. Spiritual refugees in particular hear those clichés and think, "This is why I left." They need honesty, not slogans. They need someone willing to sit in the ashes with them, not someone trying to sweep the ashes under a rug.

I'll never forget sitting at my sponsor's kitchen table in the first 30 days of my sobriety. It was a

Thursday night, and I was fragile, angry, and desperate to believe I still had some kind of spiritual credibility. He looked me dead in the eyes and said, "Ryan, this might be hard to hear, but you're spiritually disconnected." The words hit like a punch to the gut. I hated him for saying it. I was a pastor, for God's sake. I had a biblical studies degree and a Master of Divinity. If I was spiritually disconnected, then what did I even have left? In that moment, it felt like nothing, and yet that "nothing" was exactly where God began to rebuild me. Sometimes the words that feel like a death sentence are actually an invitation to new life.

Hope without the BS looks pain in the face and refuses to look away. It doesn't rush to fix or to cover up. It says, "This is awful, but this isn't all there is."

Honest Hope: Holding Pain and Possibility Together

Honest hope doesn't deny reality. It doesn't sugarcoat relapse or minimize broken trust. It doesn't pretend your loved one will be magically healed by next Tuesday. Honest hope holds both truths in tension: the wreckage is real, and so is the possibility of redemption.

This kind of hope is fierce. It's the kind of hope that keeps showing up even when it's afraid. It's gritty, not glossy. Recovery wisdom speaks to this: "One day at a time." "Progress, not perfection." Those phrases aren't cheap slogans, they are battle cries for people clawing their way back to life. They remind us that the future doesn't have to be solved all at once, and healing is possible even when it isn't fast or clean.

To those who have been burned by false promises or religious manipulation, hear this: Hope doesn't belong to those who have it all figured out. Hope is for the doubters, the exhausted, the angry, the ones who can't even pray right now. Hope is for you, too.

Naming Small Miracles

Big, dramatic turnarounds make headlines. But in real life, recovery and healing often come in small, almost invisible moments. The returned phone call you didn't expect. The day your loved one chooses honesty over hiding. The first genuine laugh you've heard from them in months. The small miracle of waking up and realizing you went one day without numbing the pain.

Noticing small miracles isn't about pretending everything is fine. It's about choosing to see life flickering in the cracks. When you name these moments, you start to build resilience. You remind yourself that despair doesn't get the final word.

And it's not just for you. Naming small miracles out loud is a gift to the community. Sometimes the person sitting next to you can't see any light for themselves, but when you speak up and say, "My daughter texted me today, just to say she was safe," or "I made it through this day without reaching for a drink," you are holding up a lantern in the dark for someone else. You're saying, "Look, hope is here, even if it's small."

Small miracles look like a son showing up late but sober to Thanksgiving dinner for the first time in years. They look like a sponsor picking up their phone on a sleepless night. They look like the addict who admits a slip instead of hiding it. They look like a mother's prayer whispered in exhaustion, or a father choosing not to yell this time but to listen instead. They're a smile across the room at FREE Recovery Community, a stranger's hug that doesn't ask for anything in return, or a boundary finally held after years of chaos.

These moments are sacred not because they are flashy, but because they are real. They are proof that God is at work in places we often overlook. They stitch courage into our bones and remind us that every step forward, no matter how small, is evidence of life pushing back against despair.

And here's the thing: we have to stop looking for God only in the big, cinematic moments. The lightning bolts. The massive conversions. The perfectly tied-up testimonies. If we wait for those, we'll miss where God is already moving. Remember the story in 1 Kings 19 where Elijah stood on the mountain, waiting for God in the shattering rocks, the roaring wind, the earthquake, and the fire but God wasn't in any of those. Then came a gentle whisper, and that's where God was. Sometimes we just miss it. God is in the quiet kitchen table conversations. God is in the ride you offered a friend when you didn't have the time. God is in the tired but brave laugh after a hard day. The ordinary is not ordinary at all. It's holy ground. Recovery teaches us that the sacred isn't always loud. Sometimes it's subtle and easily missed, hiding in the day-to-day grit of showing up.

Stop waiting for the fireworks. Look for the flicker. Pay attention to the small, stubborn signs of life around you. That's where God is. That's where hope begins to breathe again.

Speaking Hope to Addicts and Loved Ones

Hope is not a sales pitch. It is not pretending everything is okay. It is speaking words that are both true and life-giving. When you speak hope, you are not promising a quick fix or painless recovery, you are reminding someone that they are not alone and not beyond redemption.

Try words like:

"I believe you can face today, even if tomorrow feels impossible."

"You're not beyond healing, no matter what the wreckage looks like."

"This is hard, and I'm here with you."

"You're more than the worst thing you've done."

To the loved one of an addict: speaking hope to yourself matters, too. Saying, "I can't control this, but I can choose to love without enabling," is an act of hope. Saying, "I matter, even when I feel invisible," is an act of hope. Your voice deserves to be heard, both by others and by yourself.

If you've been burned by false hope before, your suspicion of hope is valid. Maybe you've been promised that this time will be different, that the relapse is the last one, that a quick prayer or a new rehab will fix everything. Maybe you've whispered to yourself, "I can't do this again," because the cost of hoping feels too high. To the addict who's tired of disappointing everyone, and to the mother, brother, partner, or friend who's watched promises shatter again and again; you are not foolish for feeling guarded. That guardedness is a scar, and scars tell the truth about where you've been.

But real hope is different. Real hope doesn't deny the wreckage or pretend the pain never happened. It doesn't offer magic formulas or perfect guarantees. Real hope breathes in the dark places. It stands with you in the middle of the mess and says, "Even here, even now, the story isn't over." Hope is gritty and unpolished. It comes through quiet acts of love: a sponsor answering the phone in the middle of the night, a friend sitting next to you in court, a small group of people choosing to show up week after week without judgment. Hope is alive, not because everything is fixed, but because even in the ruins, connection is stronger than despair.

The Spiritual Dimension of Hope

Hope is deeply spiritual, but not in the sanitized, performance-driven way many of us were taught. It is not about pretending you are fine or having perfect faith. It is about daring to believe that even in the darkest night, light is still possible.

Scripture tells us over and over that God shows up in the mess: in deserts, in prisons, on stormy seas, at gravesides. Jesus didn't offer hope from a safe distance, he walked into the chaos, sat with the outcasts, and wept with the grieving. Hope is not about earning God's attention, it is about discovering that God has been in the wreckage with you all along.

For spiritual refugees, this matters. You may have been told that doubt disqualifies you or that anger at God makes you unworthy. But your questions, your anger, your exhaustion, they are not barriers to God's presence. They are the very places where hope can break through. God is not threatened by your anger, your doubts, or your hard questions. God can handle them. Religion might be threatened by your honesty, but God is not.

Building a Culture of Hope

Hope does not survive on its own. It needs a place to breathe, a place to be spoken out loud. At FREE Recovery Community, we believe in gathering together because isolation kills hope, but connection revives it. We remind each other of the importance of celebrating one more day sober, one more boundary held, one more person walking through the door.

We also come together in times of death and darkness. Our community knows death of all kinds, overdose, alcoholism, giving up. We've stood beside caskets and hospital beds, and we've sat in living rooms where the air was thick with despair. Even in those moments, especially in those moments, we remind each other that we're in it together. You're not alone. We hold one another when the world feels too heavy to bear, and somehow, in that shared grief, hope flickers back to life.

We remind each other that we are all just a bunch of little miracles roaming around, giving each other hope, refusing to let despair have the final word. We believe God is in all of this messy, imperfect, beautiful work, right here among us, not far away waiting for us to get it together.

To the one who has been skeptical of community, skeptical of hope, skeptical of God's work in the world, you are not alone in your doubt. You do not have to come polished or certain. At FREE, we are proof that even the skeptical can find themselves surprised by grace. God shows up in the shared laughter, the shared tears, and the small, holy moments when someone says, "Me too," and you realize you are not fighting alone.

Closing Vision
Hope as a Defiant Act

Hope is not naive optimism. It is a choice to stand in the rubble and say, "This is not the end." It is refusing to let shame define the story or despair dictate the future. It is defiant, gritty, and stubborn.

Imagine a world where addicts, their families, and spiritual refugees no longer hide in shame. Where the language of hope isn't sanitized or sugarcoated but honest, raw, and alive. Where communities create spaces for healing and connection that no one has to earn.

Hope is not reserved for the strong or the saintly. It is for the doubters, the exhausted, and the brokenhearted. It is for you. It is for the one who thinks they have nothing left. Even here, even now, hope is still breathing. You can speak it, you can share it, and you can build it, brick by brick, story by story, until despair has nowhere left to hide.

Reflection Questions for Chapter 9

When has someone spoken hope to you in a way that felt raw and honest rather than sugarcoated? How did it impact you?

Where in your life or relationships could you begin to name small miracles as a way of nurturing hope?

How can you speak hope to yourself as well as to the addict or loved one you're walking alongside?

What step can you take to help build a culture of hope, in your family, friendships, or community, where shame and despair don't get the final word?

Chapter 10
Creating Space for Healing, Recovery, and Spiritual Connection

Adam's Story
Belonging That Saves Lives

Adam isn't the kind of guy most churches know what to do with. He's eight years clean and sober now, but his past is written all over him, tattoos crawl up his neck and across his face like a map of survival. He's done time in prison. He rides with a sober motorcycle club. And he drops the F-bomb like it's a comma. If you're looking for polished church language, Adam will offend you before he says hello.

But ask my wife, Tami, to name five people she trusts most in our FREE Recovery Community, and Adam will be one of them, every time.

The week before Adam shared his story as our Saturday night guest storyteller, he sat across from me in my office, nervous in a way only the truly brave are. He'd survived trauma and abuse, years of self-destruction with drugs and alcohol, and prison walls that tried to break him. He had clawed his way back to sobriety and had learned the slow, gritty work of rebuilding a life. He wasn't scared of a crowd. But he was scared of being vulnerable.

I asked him, "Why are you here at FREE? Why do you keep coming back?"

Adam looked down for a moment, then back up, his voice low but steady. "Ryan... I've done terrible things. I don't understand the Bible. But from day one here, I was told I belong. I was told this was home. I was told God loves me. And I'm actually starting to believe it."

That's belonging. It's not a slogan. It's not a clever church growth strategy. It's a lifeline.

The night Adam shared his story, he stood on our little stage, voice shaking as he walked us through his past, the trauma, the abuse, the drugs, the cells. And then, the miracle of freedom. When he finished, the room rose to its feet in a standing ovation. It wasn't for perfection. It wasn't even for survival. It was for the courage to stand in the wreckage and speak life.

Adam is often the first one through the doors now, asking how he can be of service. And here's what I've learned watching him: when people finally get who they are, that they are loved, seen, and claimed, what they do follows. Belonging changes everything.

This is the heartbeat of FREE Recovery Community: creating spaces where people who have been cast out, burned by religion, or weighed down by addiction discover that they are not alone and that grace has room for them, too.

Why Space Matters More Than Programs

Programs can be helpful. Classes, curriculums, steps, and strategies can all play a part. But space, the kind of sacred space where someone like Adam can walk in and breathe again, changes lives. People don't come to FREE because we have the slickest programming or the best coffee (though, let's be honest, we do have the best coffee). They come because they sense something real: a place where they can show up shattered, confused, angry, or skeptical and not be dismissed.

Addicts, loved ones of addicts, and spiritual refugees have been sold too many quick fixes. They've been handed easy slogans like "Just pray harder," "Think positive," "Everything happens for a reason," or "One weekend retreat will solve everything." They've been promised that a single book, a single worship service, or a single motivational talk would erase years of pain and trauma. Some were told that if their faith were strong enough, their family member wouldn't relapse, or that their own doubt made them the problem. And when those promises failed, the shame cut even deeper. These shortcuts don't just fail to heal; they leave scars.

For the mother who has sat up night after night listening for the door to creak open, for the brother who has watched a sibling self-destruct, for the spiritual refugee who walked away from church after being blamed for their own pain, you are not invisible. You are not foolish for feeling guarded or exhausted. You are seen. You are heard. You are valued.

What heals is presence, not polish. It's the open chair, the listening ear, the hug that doesn't ask for anything in return. Space tells people: you matter before you fix yourself. You belong before you believe everything.

At FREE, we've seen over and over again that when space is safe, hearts open. The addict dares to whisper the truth. The loved one dares to cry. The spiritual refugee dares to ask a question. Space is where God can do what programs alone never will.

Radical Hospitality and Welcome

Radical hospitality doesn't look like polished perfection or polite small talk. It's not about scripted greetings or surface-level pleasantries. It's a gritty, inconvenient kind of welcome that risks getting close to someone else's pain. It's sitting down next to the person who feels invisible. It's choosing to stay present when their story makes you uncomfortable or challenges your assumptions.

For addicts and their loved ones, for those who left churches because of shame or harm, hospitality is not optional, it's oxygen. A genuine welcome can disarm years of suspicion. It can crack open a heart that was slammed shut long ago.

But here's the truth: radical welcome isn't possible without authenticity. People who have survived addiction or been burned by religion can sniff out fake kindness in seconds. They've been sold masks and performance before. They don't need more of that, they need real. When you walk into a room and see people who are fully themselves, messy, imperfect, unpolished, it creates permission to breathe. Authenticity says, "You don't have to edit yourself to belong here."

At FREE, radical welcome happens because people don't have to pretend. Leaders admit their own scars. Volunteers laugh loudly, cry openly, and drop their own masks at the door. We've learned that hospitality is not about creating a flawless environment; it's about creating a truthful one. When we show up as our authentic selves, it signals to everyone else that they can, too.

This kind of welcome can be uncomfortable. It means being willing to hear stories that rattle your assumptions, to sit beside someone who doesn't look or talk like you, to risk having your own faith stretched or reshaped. But that discomfort is holy, it's where connection is born. Radical hospitality says, "I will not require you to become someone else before you can belong."

Authenticity transforms hospitality from a handshake into a lifeline. It turns a room into a refuge. And it reminds every person walking through the door: you are not here to impress, you are here to be seen.

Building Trust Through Consistency and Vulnerability

Trust doesn't come with one warm handshake or a single moving sermon. It's built in a hundred small moments: showing up, keeping your word, admitting your own flaws. In communities like FREE, many people arrive carrying scars from churches or relationships where trust was betrayed. They are watching to see if your welcome will last beyond the first hello.

Consistency says, "I'm still here when the excitement wears off." Vulnerability says, "You don't have to pretend because I'm not pretending either." When leaders risk being honest about their own wounds, it gives permission for others to stop performing and start healing.

This is slow, sometimes frustrating work. But when trust begins to grow, walls fall. The addict begins to believe that recovery might stick. The spiritual refugee starts to suspect that God hasn't abandoned them after all. And the loved one of an addict dares to hope again.

Rebuilding trust is hard, but recovery shows us it's possible. Recovery itself is proof that broken things can be made whole. When you've walked through your own darkness and experienced grace anyway, you begin to believe that trust can be earned back, not overnight, not perfectly, but piece by piece. The process is messy, but every small act of integrity, every honest word, every time you show up when you say you will, lays another brick. Recovery teaches us that trust isn't about perfection, it's about persistence.

Integrating Spiritual Connection Without Religious Baggage

Spirituality that heals doesn't bully or manipulate. It invites. It creates space for silence, questions, and doubt. It says, "Come as you are, even if you're angry, even if you're unsure." It doesn't demand that you memorize the right verses, clean yourself up, or prove your worth before you can draw near to what's holy. It understands that some people flinch at the very words "church" or "God" because those words have been weaponized against them.

This kind of spirituality doesn't hide behind polished performances or religious jargon. It meets people in kitchens, on front porches, in coffee shops, or sitting quietly in a circle of chairs where no one has to pretend. It knows that a whispered "help" is as powerful as a shouted prayer. It recognizes that a shared tear can carry as much sacred weight as any sermon. And it celebrates that discovering the sacred often happens in small, ordinary moments: a conversation that goes deeper than expected, a song lyric that cracks a hardened heart, a quiet sunrise after a sleepless night.

When we strip away the baggage, spirituality becomes less about defending doctrines and more about connecting hearts. It becomes a reminder that God is not threatened by your doubts or your anger, and that grace is big enough to hold every part of you. It allows people who've been burned by religion to breathe again and begin to believe that the sacred hasn't abandoned them.

God has been meeting people in raw, authentic places since the beginning. In Exodus, God meets Moses not in a throne room but in a burning bush on a lonely mountainside. In the Gospels, Jesus meets people on dusty roads, at dinner tables with tax collectors, beside wells with outcasts, and on stormy seas with terrified friends. The risen Christ meets his followers on an ordinary beach, cooking breakfast over a fire. Scripture keeps telling us: God shows up in the places we least expect, where we can finally lay down our baggage and be honest about our wounds. The baggage we carry, the shame, the rigid rules, the fear of not being enough, keeps us from entering those sacred spaces. Letting it go isn't about rejecting faith; it's about stepping into deeper, truer connection with God, who is already there, waiting in the mess and the ordinary.

The Power of Shared Stories and Communal Healing

Stories heal where lectures can't. They cut through shame, dismantle stereotypes, and remind us we're not alone. When someone stands up and says, "This is my wreckage, and I'm still here," it creates a holy kind of defiance against despair. Shared stories tell the addict, the loved one, and the skeptic that the worst day doesn't get the last word.

Communal healing happens when those stories echo across the room and settle in our bones. It's when the father who once swore he'd never forgive learns to unclench his fists after hearing another father talk about forgiveness. It's when the woman who thought she was too far gone recognizes herself in a story and realizes she isn't. Stories don't fix everything. But they open doors. They create possibility where there was only resignation.

Creating Rhythms That Sustain Hope

Hope doesn't survive on inspiration alone, it needs rhythms that carry it through ordinary days. Communities of healing build habits that nurture connection: shared meals, small acts of service, remembering those we've lost, celebrating milestones that might seem small to others but are monumental here, thirty days sober, a boundary held, a reconciled phone call.

These rhythms remind us that progress is rarely flashy. It's often a slow, steady heartbeat in the background of our lives. Simple practices, lighting a candle for someone struggling, pausing for silence before a meal, sending a text that says, "You're not alone," become sacred over time. They anchor hope, even when the waves keep coming.

These anchors matter most in the storms. When relapse happens, when funerals come too soon, when old wounds flare up and everything feels fragile, these small, consistent practices hold us steady. They remind us that hope isn't dependent on calm seas or perfect outcomes. Hope endures because we choose, again and again, to show up for one another, to mark the small miracles, and to keep believing that even in chaos, light still breaks through.

Closing Vision
A Table Big Enough for All of Us

Imagine a table where no one has to fake a smile to earn their seat. Picture a space where addicts, loved ones, and spiritual refugees sit side by side, where the scars, the doubts, the questions, and the messiness aren't liabilities but badges of survival. Picture a room where no one has to wonder if they belong, because belonging is the starting point, not the reward.

The world is starving for this kind of table. Too many are standing outside, pressed against windows, convinced that grace has an exclusive guest list. Too many have been turned away by churches that valued rules over people. Too many have been told they had to fix themselves before they could come home.

And this is exactly the picture Jesus paints in Luke 15 with the story of the prodigal son. The younger son takes his inheritance, squanders everything on scandalous living, and burns too many bridges. He hits bottom. He's broke, hungry, and alone. Fear keeps him from going home, he's certain he'll face shame and condemnation, but he has nowhere else to turn. So he begins the long walk back. And while he is still a long way off, the father, who represents God in the story, sees him, is filled with compassion, and runs to him. He doesn't lecture or punish. He throws a party. He calls the whole community together to celebrate because, as he says, "This son of mine was lost, but now he's home." The son didn't have to earn it. He simply showed up. That kind of love will always break through barriers of shame.

And here's the truth: grace is not scarce, and the table is not small. The invitation is wide open. And it's on us, not some distant institution, not someone else, to build it. It won't happen by accident. It takes courage to risk love, to dismantle shame, to choose connection over comfort. It takes work to look a hurting world in the eye and say, "You belong here, just as you are."

This is the urgent, holy task before us: to create communities where no one is left outside in the cold. To set tables big enough for the doubters, the angry, the broken, and the brave. To live like we actually believe that love is stronger than fear and that hope still breathes, even here, even now.

Reflection Questions for Chapter 10

Belonging and Barriers: When you think about Adam's story and the prodigal son, what barriers have kept you or someone you love from feeling like you belonged? How might a community of radical welcome begin to dismantle those barriers?

Programs vs. Presence: Reflect on a time when presence mattered more than polished programs in your own life. How can you personally help create sacred spaces where people can show up as they are without needing to perform?

Authenticity and Trust: Why do you think authenticity and vulnerability are essential for trust to grow? What small, practical steps could you take to build trust with someone who has been burned by religion or relationships?

Creating a Bigger Table: Imagine your own "bigger table." Who would you invite to sit beside you, even if it felt uncomfortable? What risks are you willing to take to build or participate in a community where no one is left outside in the cold?

Chapter 11
Spaces of Radical Welcome

When the Door Is Completely New
Welcoming the Unfamiliar

Several years ago, I stood at the front of a crowded room, officiating the funeral of a young man who had died of a drug overdose. The air was heavy, the kind of heaviness you can feel in your chest. His parents were shattered. His childhood photos lined a table at the back of the room, snapshots of baseball uniforms, goofy grins, and family camping trips that now felt like a different lifetime.

Outside on the sidewalk, a group of his friends clustered together, smoking cigarettes like lifelines. They weren't hardened church critics or angry ex-Christians. Most of them had never been inside a church building in their lives. They weren't carrying stories of being shamed from a pulpit or excluded by a congregation. They were carrying something quieter: uncertainty. They didn't know what to do, how to act, or if they belonged.

I watched as they hesitated at the doors, one of them asking in a whisper, "Are we even allowed in?" Another fidgeted with his lighter, glancing at the stained-glass windows like they might be alarm systems. It wasn't rebellion that held them back; it was fear, fear of being judged, fear of sticking out, fear of not knowing the unspoken rules. They weren't sure if they were dressed right, if they'd stand at the wrong time, or if someone might glare at the smell of smoke on their jackets.

When they finally stepped inside, their eyes darted around the room, searching for cues on how to behave. Some of them kept to the back, shoulders hunched, like they were apologizing for even being there. In that moment, I was struck by a hard truth: many spiritual refugees aren't angry at the church, they're simply unfamiliar. They don't arrive with baggage to unpack; they arrive with questions, doubt, and the aching desire to grieve their friend without feeling out of place.

That day reminded me that radical welcome isn't only for the people burned by religion. It's also for those who have never crossed a church threshold before. If the body of Christ, or any community of healing, can't make room for people like them, people standing on the sidewalk, trembling with uncertainty, then we are failing the very mission we claim to carry.

Beyond Two Hours on Sunday
Space That Heals All Week

Radical welcome doesn't start and stop between the opening song and the final benediction. A space of healing isn't defined by a two-hour window on a Sunday morning, it's built in the ordinary hours of the week. Healing happens in the quiet phone calls at midnight, the text that says "I'm thinking of you," and the moments of laughter that break through tears on a Wednesday afternoon.

If the doors are closed, literally or figuratively, when those moments come, people learn that church isn't where you bring your real life. (And just to keep us honest, FREE meets on Saturday nights, not Sundays. We like to joke that God shows up just as powerfully on Saturdays and that coffee tastes better without a Sunday morning alarm clock.)

At FREE, we're open throughout the week. Our coffee shop is open to the public, and it is often the first face of our community that people encounter. Sometimes the space we create is quite literal: a warm, welcoming room where the smell of fresh coffee meets them before their shame does. And when they walk through that door, it's a peer, not a superior, who greets them, listens to their story, and reminds them they belong. This small, tangible space ties directly into our mission: breaking the silence of addiction while creating space for healing, recovery, and spiritual connection.

That mission is our anchor and our filter. It tells us what to say yes to and what to say no to. Without it, we risk filling calendars with activity that looks busy but doesn't heal. Mission clarity prevents burnout and builds trust. It keeps you grounded when opportunities or challenges tempt you to scatter your energy. When every gathering, event, or conversation flows from the mission, the community senses consistency, and hope begins to grow roots.

For faith leaders, this isn't just about scheduling more events. It's about aligning every effort, whether it's a recovery group, a social gathering, or an honest conversation, to the deeper purpose of being a space where the hurting find healing and connection. When the mission drives the space, it's not just an event on a calendar, it's a living, breathing refuge that says: you are not alone.

United by Mission, Not Uniformity

Radical welcome doesn't demand agreement on every religious, political, or philosophical issue. It doesn't require everyone to see the world the same way or recite the same creeds. What binds a true community together isn't sameness, it's mission.

In spaces of healing, you'll find people who vote differently, believe differently, and think differently. But if they are united by a shared mission to break the silence of addiction, to create spaces for recovery and spiritual connection, to love people where they are, then those differences become strengths rather than threats.

This doesn't mean conversations will always be comfortable. Disagreements will happen. Questions will surface. Sometimes they will sting. Sometimes they will leave you wondering if you even belong in the same room. But this is the hard, holy work of community: staying at the table when it would be easier to walk away. Refusing to let disagreement fracture the mission. Choosing, even in discomfort, to lean toward each other instead of away.

For addicts, loved ones of addicts, and spiritual refugees, this matters deeply. You already know what it feels like to be cut off, to be told you don't belong, to be treated as a problem to be fixed or a burden to be managed. The world has done enough excluding. The only way forward is to walk hand-in-hand toward a common goal, even when it's messy. This is what makes hope credible, it isn't neat or painless. It's gritty, defiant love that says, "We will not let differences keep us from healing together."

When a recovering addict and a spiritual refugee can sit beside a lifelong churchgoer and all three find hope at the same table, that's the kingdom of God breaking through. Unity built on mission doesn't erase identity or conviction, it weaves them together into something beautiful. It's a quiet but powerful rebellion against a world that keeps drawing lines and demanding sides. It tells the watching world: you can belong here even before you believe, and even if you never believe exactly like us.

Reflection Questions for Chapter 11

Welcoming the Unfamiliar: Have you ever been in a space where you weren't sure how to act or if you belonged? What did you feel in that moment, and what might have helped you step through the door sooner?

Mission as a Filter: In what ways can your community's mission act as a guide for what to say yes to or no to? How might this clarity create more intentional healing spaces?

Diversity and Mission: How have you seen unity around a shared mission overcome differences in worldview or belief? What challenges and opportunities can arise from this diversity?

Your Role in Radical Welcome: What is one tangible step you can take this week to extend radical welcome to someone unfamiliar with spiritual or recovery spaces?

Chapter 12
Practices That Stick

Ethan's Story: Small Steps Save Lives

Ethan sat on the edge of his mattress, the kind that had seen too many nights on too many floors. The clock on his phone glowed 5:14 a.m. He hadn't slept much, but this was different from the nights when vodka kept him awake. This time, it was the weight of staying sober. Day three. His head pounded. His hands shook. And the thought of the whole day stretched out in front of him felt like standing at the base of a mountain with no gear, no map, and no chance.

The voices in his head were merciless. You'll never make it. You've screwed it all up too many times. Why even bother? He almost reached for the bottle he'd stashed under the sink, except he remembered it wasn't there anymore. He'd dumped it last night, angry and desperate, then cried when he realized how much of himself was wrapped up in that empty bottle.

Then, through the haze of panic, he remembered what the guy at the meeting had said: "Just start small. Make your bed. Drink some water. Call one person." It sounded ridiculous. But he had nothing else. So he tugged the blanket over the mattress, crooked and lumpy but finished. He drank a glass of water. Then he picked up the phone and dialed the number scribbled on the back of a grocery receipt.

The man on the other end answered groggily, but his voice softened when he heard Ethan's trembling. "You did the right thing calling," he said. "This is how it starts." Ethan didn't feel like anything was starting. He felt broken, ashamed, and exhausted. But a tiny, almost invisible thread of hope wound its way through the despair. He didn't have to conquer the whole mountain today. He just had to take the next small step.

That morning didn't look like triumph. There were no fireworks, no instant transformation. But it was a beginning, and beginnings, no matter how small, have a way of saving lives.

Building Healthy Habits That Work for You
Recovery and spiritual growth are rarely built on massive, dramatic leaps. They're built on small, consistent habits that anchor you when everything else feels shaky. The world sells the idea that transformation has to be flashy or immediate, a viral moment, a perfect prayer, a single mountaintop experience that fixes everything. But that's a lie that keeps too many people stuck.

The truth is, building habits that stick is about finding what actually works for you, not what worked for the person next to you or the influencer on social media. Some people find their center through morning prayer or reading scripture. Others find it in silent meditation, journaling, or a walk through the neighborhood at sunset. Maybe it's music, breathing exercises, or gathering weekly with a few trusted friends to be honest about the mess. The form doesn't matter as much as the consistency and authenticity.

For spiritual refugees, this matters even more. You don't have to inherit the exact practices of a tradition that wounded you. You don't have to light the same candles or recite the same words if they feel like chains instead of lifelines. You are free to build habits that connect you to what is meaningful and healing. The goal isn't to replicate someone else's formula, it's to create space where your soul can breathe.

Healthy habits are more than boxes to check, they're lifelines. They pull you back to center when life's chaos threatens to drag you under. They teach you that showing up matters even when you don't feel like it. Over time, these rhythms create stability where there used to be crisis. They slowly rewire your mind to trust that hope is possible. A good habit can be the thing that keeps you sober on a bad day, the thread that ties you back to community when shame tells you to isolate, or the moment that reminds you God hasn't gone anywhere.

Here are some habits to consider as you build your own:

Gratitude Practice: Write down three things you're grateful for each day, even on the days when gratitude feels impossible.

Daily Check-In: Text or call a trusted friend or mentor to honestly share how you're doing.

Quiet Reflection or Prayer: Set aside five minutes to breathe, reflect, or speak to God, even if all you can say is "help."

Scripture or Sacred Reading: Read a short passage from scripture or another meaningful text, not as a chore but as nourishment.

Acts of Kindness: Do one small, intentional act of kindness every day, even if no one notices.

Movement: Go for a walk, stretch, or do a simple exercise to reconnect your body and mind.

End-of-Day Review: Before bed, pause to notice one moment where light broke through, however small.

Remember Ethan's story: it wasn't a grand gesture that saved him, it was a crookedly made bed, a glass of water, and a phone call. Small steps like these can save lives.

And here's the thing: your habits can change over time. What anchors you in year one of recovery may not serve you in year five. That's okay. The point is to keep showing up, to keep experimenting, and to give yourself grace. Even small, imperfect habits are acts of resistance against despair. They are declarations that your life is worth tending to.

Serving Others as Spiritual Practice

There comes a point in recovery and in spiritual growth where turning inward isn't enough. Healing starts inside you, but it never stays there. Serving others is not just a nice add-on or a box to check, it is a lifeline that keeps you grounded and reminds you that your pain can become purpose.

Serving cuts through self-absorption, that voice in your head that says everything is hopeless or all about you. When you pour a cup of coffee for someone else, offer a ride, clean up a meeting space, or simply ask someone how they're really doing, you are declaring that your story isn't just about your wounds. You are saying, "I am part of something bigger."

At FREE, we are constantly asked about volunteer opportunities. People don't line up to serve because they're chasing recognition or want someone to tell them how great they are. They step forward because they know what's at stake. They know that serving others is the way out of their own heads, the way to silence shame's whisper that says they don't matter. They know it's one of the things that keeps them sober. I've watched people in early recovery wipe down tables, stack chairs, or welcome newcomers at the coffee shop, and I've seen the light come back into their eyes as they realize: "This matters. I matter."

Service has a way of getting us out of ourselves. It breaks the illusion that our pain or our situation is entirely unique. It reminds us of our common bond, that we all carry wounds, that we all need each other, and that none of us are beyond redemption. Serving pulls us out of isolation and places us back into the human family where grace is alive and moving.

Serving others actually saves us. It's not about polishing your reputation or earning God's favor, it's about creating space for grace to move through you. It's a spiritual practice that deepens your path, re-centers your priorities, and heals wounds you didn't even know you were still carrying.

Jesus modeled this perfectly. He washed the dirty feet of his friends, touched people others avoided, and fed crowds without asking for credentials. He didn't use service as a way to prove worthiness; he used it as a way to communicate love. When we serve, we echo that kind of radical love.

Serving doesn't have to be glamorous. It doesn't have to be big. It can look like picking up chairs after a gathering, sending an encouraging text to someone who's struggling, or offering a listening ear without judgment. And here's the secret: when you serve, you often end up being the one who's healed a little more.

A Marathon, Not a Sprint
No Finish Lines in Recovery or Faith

If you're looking for a quick fix, recovery will break your heart. Faith will, too. Neither offers medals for perfect attendance or a finish line where you can finally say, "I've arrived." The spiritual life and the recovery journey are marathons with no final tape to break, they are lifelong, evolving paths.

This truth can feel frustrating, especially when you're exhausted. We want milestones that prove we're "done," that we've conquered the chaos. But the reality is, there's no arrival point where life suddenly becomes painless or effortless. There are stretches of road where you'll feel strong, and there will be hills that feel endless. Some days you'll feel like you're sprinting; other days you'll barely crawl forward. Both count. Forward is forward.

For addicts, loved ones of addicts, and spiritual refugees, this is freeing if you let it be. You don't have to live under the pressure of perfection or fear that one stumble erases your progress. Relapse, doubt, or setbacks don't disqualify you, they remind you that the race is still being run and you're still in it. There's no scoreboard, no medals handed out for having the cleanest story. What matters is that you keep showing up, one step at a time. And when you keep showing up, something powerful happens: you begin to pass the gift forward. A core recovery principle teaches us that to keep the gift, you must give it away. Your presence, your story, and your willingness to serve become lifelines for others who are still unsure if hope is real. Every time you show up, whether it's to pour coffee, offer a hug, or simply listen, you are keeping your own hope alive by planting it in someone else.

Think of the long-distance runner: they pace themselves, hydrate, and rest when needed. They don't burn out trying to sprint the entire course. Likewise, you don't have to "win" at recovery or spirituality, you just have to stay in the game. Celebrate the small wins: the day you chose to reach out instead of isolate, the moment you forgave yourself a little faster, the boundary you kept even when it hurt.

And here's the grace in all of it: God walks this marathon with you. Even when you doubt, even when you're angry or numb, even when you're crawling on your hands and knees, you are not alone on the course. Hope isn't waiting for you at the finish line, it's running beside you right now.

Reflection Questions for Chapter 12

Small Beginnings: Think about Ethan's story of making his bed, drinking water, and making a call. What small, simple habit could you start today that might anchor you when life feels overwhelming?

Habits That Anchor You: Which practices, spiritual or practical, have helped you feel grounded in the past? Are there habits you've avoided because of fear, shame, or past experiences with religion? What might experimenting with new or reimagined habits look like for you now?

Serving as Survival: Reflect on a time when helping someone else shifted your own perspective or softened your pain. How might stepping out to serve, even in a small way, create healing for you today?

Marathon Mentality: Where are you tempted to look for a finish line in your recovery or spiritual journey? What would it mean to embrace this as a marathon instead of a sprint, and to keep showing up even when progress feels slow or uncertain?

Chapter 13
Staying in the Game for the Long Haul

The Long Arc of Healing

Caleb hadn't prayed in fifteen years. Not since the night he'd walked out of a church basement meeting and sworn he'd never step inside a religious space again. Too many broken promises, too many sideways glances, too many sermons that felt like accusations. Faith, as far as Caleb was concerned, was a game for people who could fake it better than he could.

But addiction has a way of stripping a person bare. After another relapse, another job lost, and another friend who stopped returning calls, Caleb found himself sitting in a recovery meeting one Tuesday night, trying not to look anyone in the eye. The room was loud with laughter and coffee cups clinking, but the sound felt foreign. When it came time for people to share, a woman across the circle spoke with a kind of honesty Caleb didn't recognize. She didn't sugarcoat her pain. She didn't pretend she had it all together. She said, "I was done. Completely done. But grace met me in a place I didn't expect. It wasn't the grace of polished sermons or perfect people. It was the grace of a phone call at midnight and a stranger who said, 'You're not alone.'"

Something cracked open in Caleb. It wasn't a blinding light or a booming voice from heaven. It was small, like a door creaking open after years of being stuck. He didn't pray that night, but he stayed after the meeting to help stack chairs. And when someone invited him to coffee the next morning, he said yes, even though every part of him wanted to run. That coffee led to another meeting, which led to an evening where Caleb, for the first time in years, whispered a clumsy, awkward prayer.

Caleb didn't find a religion that night. What he found was a flicker of faith, a sense that maybe God hadn't walked away after all. Recovery had become the doorway back to a spiritual connection he thought he'd burned forever. It wasn't neat, and it wasn't instant. But it was real. And real was enough to start again.

Caleb's story isn't unique. It's the quiet miracle happening in recovery rooms, coffee shops, and whispered conversations every single day. The long arc of healing rarely looks like a straight line. It looks more like scribbles on a page, progress mixed with setbacks, tears mingled with laughter, moments of grace hidden inside ordinary days. Healing is messy, and yet it's in the mess that hope keeps breaking through.

Too often, we imagine recovery or spiritual growth as a series of clear milestones: get sober, find faith, clean up the wreckage, live happily ever after. But life doesn't unfold like a clean narrative. The long arc of healing stretches across years, and sometimes decades. There will be seasons where faith feels alive and electric and seasons where it feels silent. There will be stretches where sobriety feels steady and other stretches where temptation whispers louder than ever.

What makes the difference is not perfection, but persistence. Healing isn't about never falling, it's about refusing to stay down. It's about stacking chairs when you'd rather run, answering the phone when you're ashamed, praying awkward prayers when you're not sure you believe anymore. The long arc is about showing up again and again, trusting that even small acts of courage accumulate into transformation.

For addicts, loved ones of addicts, and spiritual refugees, this truth matters. Maybe you're in a dry season where God feels distant. Maybe you're rebuilding trust after relapse or after years of doubting your worth. Maybe you've walked away from faith entirely and are only just now peeking through the doorway again. You are not disqualified. The long arc of healing is wide enough to hold your story.

The long arc also reminds us that grace isn't a one-time transaction, it's an ongoing companion. The God who welcomed the prodigal son while he was still far off is the same God who waits, walks, and whispers through every relapse, every tear, and every hesitant return. Grace doesn't demand that you have it all together. Grace just asks you to keep taking steps, however small, toward connection with God, with yourself, and with others.

Pacing Yourself
Avoiding Burnout and Isolation

Burnout is one of the quiet killers of recovery and faith. It doesn't usually announce itself with a crash, it creeps in slowly. It shows up as exhaustion you can't shake, resentment toward the people you're trying to love, or the whisper that none of it matters anyway. When you're worn thin, isolation starts to look tempting. Pulling away feels safer than risking more disappointment.

But isolation is dangerous territory. Addiction, despair, and shame all thrive in the dark. When you drift too far from connection, the old lies get louder: You're alone. Nobody cares. You'll never change. Pacing yourself isn't weakness; it's wisdom. It's knowing that you can't fix every problem, save every person, or attend every event without eventually breaking yourself.

At FREE, we talk a lot about balance. It's tempting, especially after an early rush of hope, to throw yourself into every opportunity, to serve at every gathering, take every call, and be the one who never says no. But overextending doesn't honor the mission, and it doesn't honor your own healing. Healthy boundaries are not selfish; they are sacred. They make it possible for you to keep showing up over the long haul.

Pacing yourself also means building rhythms of rest. Find moments to breathe, laugh, and do things that refill your soul. Let a trusted friend or mentor know when you're running on empty. Reach out before the burnout becomes a spiral. Rest doesn't mean quitting; it means remembering you're human.

And when you feel the pull to isolate, when shame tells you that you're too broken or too tired, resist the urge to disappear. The very moment you want to withdraw is the moment you most need community.

Keep showing up, even if it's imperfectly. Even if all you can do is sit quietly in a chair and listen.

Passing It On
Hope Carriers in a Hurting World

One of the deepest truths of recovery is this: to keep the gift, you have to give it away. Hope is not meant to be hoarded. It grows when it's shared. When you've walked through darkness and found even a flicker of light, you carry something the world desperately needs.

Passing on hope doesn't require a pulpit or a perfect story. It doesn't mean you need to have all the answers or a polished testimony. It's found in the quiet choices: picking up the phone to check on someone, sitting beside a friend at a meeting, or simply telling the truth about your own scars. Sometimes, the most powerful sermon is a trembling voice saying, "Me too. I've been there."

At FREE, I've watched people who once swore they had nothing to offer become the very ones who hold others together. A guy who thought he was beyond redemption now stands at the door every week greeting newcomers. A woman who once hated herself now makes the coffee that fuels our conversations. None of them set out to be heroes, they just showed up, again and again, and let grace work through their ordinary actions.

This kind of passing it on isn't glamorous. It won't make headlines or earn applause. But it's what keeps communities alive. It's what breaks cycles of despair. When you show up for someone else, you remind them, and yourself, that hope is real.

And to the loved ones of addicts: your story matters just as much. The nights you spent staring at the ceiling, the prayers you whispered through tears, the boundaries you set even when your heart shattered, these are not wasted. There is another mother, brother, or partner out there who feels just as helpless, just as angry, just as ashamed. When you speak your truth, you give them a lifeline. You remind them that they are not alone, that their pain isn't proof of failure, and that love, even when bruised and battered, can still be a force for healing. Your solidarity with other loved ones may be the thing that keeps them standing when the weight feels unbearable.

The world is heavy with division, despair, and noise. Addicts, loved ones of addicts, and spiritual refugees know this better than most. But when we choose to be hope carriers, when we bring kindness where there was judgment, presence where there was abandonment, and honesty where there were lies, we become evidence that another way is possible.

Your scars can become someone else's survival guide. Your story, imperfect and unfinished, might be the very thing that keeps another person alive tonight. You don't have to fix them. You don't have to save them. You just have to show up and offer what was once offered to you: the assurance that nobody has to walk alone.

Closing Vision
The Wreckage and the Wonder

Look around, this world is messy. Addiction leaves wreckage in its wake: broken families, empty bank accounts, shattered trust, and quiet shame hiding behind polite smiles. Faith communities have their own wreckage too, wounds inflicted by judgment, exclusion, and silence. The mess is undeniable. But the wonder is here, too. It is in the fact that even in the rubble, people keep reaching for each other. They keep showing up, even bruised and afraid. They keep choosing love over bitterness, grace over shame, and connection over isolation.

The wonder is in the circle of people holding hands at a meeting, in a hug offered to someone who thought they were untouchable, in a cup of coffee shared between two people who were strangers yesterday. It's in the moment someone whispers, "Me too," and another person realizes they are not crazy, not alone, not beyond redemption.

The wreckage doesn't get the final word. Grace does. Compassion does. Community does. God does. The God who runs to embrace the prodigal child is still running toward us, toward you, right now. And God isn't waiting for you to clean yourself up or get your theology perfect. God meets you in the middle of the wreckage and dares you to believe that wonder is possible again.

This is an invitation: Keep showing up. Keep telling the truth. Keep building communities where nobody has to walk alone. Choose the small steps that lead toward connection. Be the one who reminds someone else that despair doesn't own the future. Because the wonder isn't somewhere far off, it's here, scattered through the wreckage, waiting for us to notice.

Reflection Questions for Chapter 13

The Long Arc of Healing: Where in your life do you need to embrace the slow, messy, ongoing nature of healing instead of demanding instant results?

Burnout and Balance: In what ways might you need to pace yourself better to avoid burnout or isolation? Who could you reach out to for support?

Passing Hope Forward: Who in your life might need to hear your story, not as a polished speech but as a lifeline of solidarity and grace?

Choosing Wonder in the Wreckage: When you look at the broken places around you, where can you also see wonder, small signs of grace and connection that invite you to keep going?